Adventures in
CROCHETING

by the same author

ADVENTURES IN KNITTING

KNITTING MADE EASY

Adventures in
CROCHETING

More Than 100 Easy-to-Make Patterns

With Photographs, Drawings

and Detailed Instructions

BARBARA AYTES

1972

Doubleday & Company, Inc.

Garden City, New York

PHOTOGRAPHY

Daniel Waggoner of Danick Studio, Granada Hills, California

ILLUSTRATED ITEMS CROCHETED BY

Barbara Mark, Bess Braun and the author

PET COAT MODEL

Bridget Aytes

Preface

With crocheting and the needle arts now at an all-time high in popularity, there are hundreds of good books extant on these subjects, and this is as it should be. Some contain hundreds of pattern stitches, gleaned from every possible source, and some are project oriented, containing many items and few pattern stitches.

While both formats are interesting and have an important place in one's library of needlework books, there is a third format which seems to me to strike a happy medium between those books which are full of pattern stitches and nothing to make, and those which are full of items to make and few or no pattern stitches, with which the reader may fashion her own designs and creations.

This third format, which I prefer and adhere to as much as possible, is one in which there are old favorite pattern stitches, new variations of other old favorites, and brand-new designs never before published anywhere, liberally laced throughout with items to make and suggestions by which the reader is encouraged to create her own designs.

In the following pages you will find old favorite pattern stitches, a large collection of brand-new ones designed especially for this book, and many items to make. Most of the items herein are what I am pleased to call easy-shape patterns; that is, there is no complicated shaping and, where possible, no shaping at all. Garments made of basic or very plain crochet can be embellished with costume jewelry, bright-colored scarves or yarn flowers (Part V). On the other hand, when clothing is made from some of the very unusual and interesting pattern stitches herein, the pattern stitch itself becomes the style, and it should not be obscured or belabored by complicated styling known as high fashion, which usually enjoys so short a period of popularity that it is often out of style before it is finished. Most certainly an item lovingly made by hand over a period of weeks or months, and with it a joyous anticipation of the item finished, should be of such simple lines that it will stay in style until it has worn out.

Afghans are the all-time favorite item of the vast legion of crochet hobbyists, and the limitation of space within the pages of this book prevents me from making an afghan from every new pattern stitch and joined motif in Parts III and IV. Instead, I have chosen simply to show a close-up sample of the many suitable afghan patterns, together with suggestions for using. Most readers will be able to visualize an afghan from the pattern photograph and perhaps add a few individual touches of their own.

It is literally impossible to describe and suggest every kind of yarn on the market today. I have, therefore, used the most easily obtainable types of yarn in the items herein. The amounts of different brands of yarn also vary considerably, so that although the amount given may be a few ounces more than is actually required for an individual tension or a very small size, one will always have enough yarn of one dye lot to finish an item.

On the other hand, it is almost impossible to give exact amounts and specific directions for all the suitable types of yarn one may use for stoles, dresses, afghans, etc. The needlework instructor in one's local yarn shop is always very knowledgeable in the matter of amounts of yarn required for any given item in a particular brand or type of yarn. Of course, it is not always possible for a reader to reach a yarn counter or an instructor to advise her. In this case, I will be more than happy to give specific types and brands of yarn used herein, together with the approximate amounts necessary for an item made in a pattern stitch in the following pages for which there is no specific directions or amounts given. Information of this nature can be obtained by sending an inquiry to me in care of Doubleday & Co., Inc., Garden City, New York 11530.

It was with the utmost pleasure that this book was written, and I sincerely hope that the crochet hobbyists using the patterns in this book find as much joy in fashioning them as I found in designing them.

BARBARA AYTES

Contents

Illustrations

DIAGRAMS

Abbreviations

ch	chain
sc	single crochet
hdc	half double crochet
dc	double crochet
tr	treble crochet
st(s)	stitch(es)
oz	ounce
"	inch(es)

Only the above abbreviations are used throughout the following pages. For complete clarity, all other words and phrases in connection with crocheting are unabbreviated.

ASTERISK*

A symbol used before and after a set of directions that is to be repeated across a row of crochet. For example, "*sc in next st, dc in each of next 2 sts.* Repeat between *'s across row" would be an instruction to single crochet in a stitch and double crochet in next 2 stitches across an entire row, or to within a number of stitches of end of row, in which case instructions would follow for ending the row.

Part I: *THE BASICS OF CROCHET*

Yarns

In spite of its name, the yarn known as knitting worsted is the most popular with the crochet hobbyist. Almost universally available, it works up very quickly, holds its shape through dozens of launderings and dry cleanings, and turns out a myriad of handsome items such as stoles, cardigans, blouses, vests, pullovers and dresses, as well as decorative and useful household articles such as afghans, pillows, scatter rugs, wall hanging, draperies, upholstery fabrics and the like.

Depending upon the article being made, crochet hooks used with single-strand knitting worsted range from steel sizes ⚭1, 0 and 00 through aluminum or plastic sizes F, G, H, and occasionally a loosely worked fabric will call for sizes as large as I, J and K.

For lightweight items such as spring and summer wear, the yarns known as sports, fingering and sock-and-sweater are the most useful. These three terms sometimes overlap, depending on the company producing them. Crochet hooks used with these yarns are usually steel sizes ⚭4, 3, 2, 1, 0 and 00.

Extra-fine yarns such as baby wool and two-ply shetland are most frequently worked with steel sizes ⚭7, 6, 5, 4, 3, 2, 1 and 0.

There are hundreds of novelty yarns on the market of varying weights and plies. Any suitable yarn of this kind can be substituted for the standard yarns if they yield the same stitch gauge as the yarn called for in any specific set of directions. This is extremely important in obtaining a proper fit when making clothing. It is less important in making household items where no absolute size is required; for example, the size of an afghan crocheted in small squares and set together can be controlled by adding an extra row, or omitting a row when the desired size has been obtained.

The yarns known as "bulky" or "superbulky" are produced in wool, cotton and synthetics, and are made in several sizes, again depending on the company making them. Crochet hooks used for these may vary from steel ⚭00 to aluminum and plastic sizes F through K. The wool bulky yarns are ideal for scatter rugs, heavy winter coats and jackets, hats, caps, handbags, wall hangings, etc.

The cotton bulky yarns should not be confused with what is known as crochet thread or bedspread cotton. These are fine threads and cannot be considered yarns, so when a set of directions calls for "cotton yarn," it refers to the heavier types used for pot holders, scatter rugs, hot mats,

3

and other utilitarian items which necessarily must be made of a yarn which will yield a thick, heavy fabric.

The heaviest weight cotton yarn is usually called "heavy rug cotton" in directions and is frequently so designated on the label. This is used mainly for rugs and heavy mats.

A cotton yarn of slightly lighter weight is usually called "all-purpose cotton yarn" in directions and frequently on labels. Crochet hook sizes for use with this yarn range from steel ✕0 and 00 through plastic and aluminum sizes F and G.

All-purpose cotton yarn is also suitable for rugs and many other items such as hot mats, pot holders, place setting mats, upholstery fabrics, caps, hats, tote bags, slippers, belts, pillows, stuffed animals and other novelties.

COTTON CROCHET THREAD

Cotton crochet thread is made in many sizes, from the very finest which is numbered 100 through varying degrees of thickness and numbered downward, as the thread becomes heavier, in gradations of ten. Size 90 is almost imperceptibly heavier than size 100, size 60 would be considerably heavier than size 90, size 30 would be heavier than size 60, etc.

The sizes of thread from 100 through 40 have been all but abandoned by cotton companies in the United States in recent years, and have been substituted by a product called "tatting cotton," which is about number 70 in the above size ranges and strikes a happy medium for the accommodation of tatters and crocheters who still wish to work very fine lace edgings, doilies and runners in the Victorian manner.

For the most part, crochet hobbyists at the present time prefer heavier threads which work up quickly. Sizes 30, 20 and 10 are the most popular for lacy place setting mats, edgings and tablecloths, while the heavier "pearl cotton," ranging in single digit gradations from size 5 through 1, is suitable for these same items when a heavier fabric is desired. Pearl cotton is also suitable for such articles as baby caps and bootees, pot holders, head scarves, etc.

Crochet thread labeled "bedspread cotton" (generally about size 10 or 20) is so labeled by almost every company producing it. It is made, of course, primarily for bedspreads, but serves many purposes when worked in single, double and triple strand. It is easily obtainable in almost every variety and department store and can be substituted in multiple strands for almost any set of directions calling for quick-crochet cotton, so long as enough strands are used together to obtain the proper stitch gauge.

Quick-crochet cotton, so called, is a recent innovation to accommodate those crocheters who wish to make items very quicky without having to use bedspread cotton in multiple strand. It has no number but is always labeled "quick-crochet cotton" or similar. This type of cotton is of an ex-

4

tremely hard twist with unusually long wearing ability, and is suitable for hot mats, pot holders, slippers, casual shoe tops, place setting mats, hats, caps, tote bags and many other items.

Crochet hooks ⚬0, 00 and F are usually used with single-strand quick-crochet cotton thread.

Stitch Gauge

The number of stitches to an inch of fabric sometimes varies widely. This variance is usually due to the fact that the working yarn is held at a firm tension by some and at a loose tension by others.

At the beginning of most crochet directions, particularly for any type of garment, a stitch gauge for the yarn and hook is given. Following the hook size, there is usually advice to the crocheter to use any size hook required to obtain the proper stitch gauge.

If the stitch gauge varies from the one specified in any given set of directions, the garment is likely to turn out ill fitting, either too large or too small. To avoid this, a stitch-gauge swatch should be made, using the specified yarn and hook size, before the item in question is started.

Crochet a stitch-gauge swatch by working across enough stitches so that the swatch will measure 3" or 4" wide. Work in the specified pattern until swatch measures about 3½" from the beginning. Smooth the swatch by steam pressing lightly on the reverse side. This will generally reveal a more true stitch gauge than when it is left unpressed to be measured.

Using a metal tape measure or ruler, measure the exact number of stitches to 1" of fabric, then measure across a 2" horizontal area to determine if the number of stitches per inch is an average one. If half the number of stitches in the 2" gauge is the same as the 1" gauge, and if this gauge is the correct one for a specified article, then your stitch gauge is probably an average one for the particular type of yarn used.

If a stitch-gauge swatch yields FEWER stitches per inch than are required in a given set of directions, use a SMALLER hook to obtain the proper number of stitches per inch of fabric. If a stitch-gauge swatch yields MORE stitches per inch than are required, use a LARGER hook to obtain the proper number of stitches.

Sometimes, in addition to giving a horizontal-stitch gauge, a vertical-row gauge is given. More often than not, this vertical-row gauge is not necessary, inasmuch as most expanses of crocheted fabric are measured vertically in inches rather than in rows, and has little significance in directions except where a vertical expanse of fabric is measured in row or pattern units rather than inches.

Blocking

Blocking a crocheted item is not always necessary. Frequently a light steam pressing on the reverse side of the fabric is all that is necessary. Occasionally, however, a garment will turn out just a little too snug for comfort or personal preference. This problem can be overcome by blocking to exact desired measurements, in separate pieces or after it is assembled, as follows: Assemble a supply of rustproof pins, a metal tape measure, a supply of terry-cloth towels and a blocking board.

A blocking board can be a softwood, kitchen cutting board, an old card table into which pins can be pushed, a large piece of framed fiberboard (available at most building supply stores), or any similar board with a large flat surface.

First, make sure that the item to be blocked is washable, then wet thoroughly in lukewarm water. Lift out of water using both hands (never pick up wet crocheted fabric by an edge or corner), and gently squeeze excess moisture out without wringing or twisting. Roll in a terry-cloth towel and leave for a few minutes so that the absorbent toweling can take up additional moisture. Unroll and remove item from towel, again using both hands to lift the wet fabric.

Place the wet item on the blocking board. Gently smooth out to exact desired measurements, using the metal tape measure. If you are blocking a garment, be sure to allow at least an inch or two more than actual body measurements, depending upon how snug or loose fitting you wish the finished garment to be. Pin the item firmly to the blocking board with rustproof pins, placing each pin approximately 1½″ to 2″ apart. Cover with dry terry-cloth towels and allow item to dry thoroughly, 24 to 36 hours, before removing from board. When blocking or laundering crocheted items containing more than one color of yarn, it is advisable to use 1 or 2 tablespoonfuls of white vinegar in the last rinse water. This will prevent the various colors from running while still damp.

How to Crochet

SLIP LOOP: All crocheted fabric is started with a chain as the first row, or edge, and the chain is begun with a slip loop, which is made as follows: Draw about 5″ of yarn from skein and fold in half. Twist folded end once to the right, then draw skein end of yarn through this loop (made by right twist). Pull free end of yarn downward to tighten and reduce slip loop to desired size.

CHAIN STITCH: Make a slip loop; insert hook through slip loop, wrap yarn around hook from back to front, draw yarn through. Repeat for desired length or as instructed in specific directions.

TO FORM A CHAIN RING: Make as many chain stitches as are called for in specific directions. Insert hook in first chain made, making sure that it is inserted through the lower stationary strand of slip loop (first chain) so that the cut end strand will not pull out. Wrap yarn around hook from back to front. Draw yarn through both the chain and the loop on hook. This is a slip stitch to join a chain to form a ring. This is used when an item or pattern is begun at the center, such as the tam (Part II) and the many motifs in Part IV.

SLIP STITCH: Insert hook in top of next stitch, grasp working yarn with hook, and draw through both the stitch and the loop on hook. This is ordinarily used as the last (or finishing) stitch on an expanse of fabric, a completed item or a motif.

FOUNDATION ROW FOR SINGLE CROCHET: Skip first chain. *Insert hook through next chain, wrap yarn around hook and draw loop through chain. Wrap yarn around hook and draw yarn through both loops on hook.* Repeat between *'s across chain or as instructed in specific directions. This creates a foundation row on which to work a single crochet fabric and various patterns.

HALF DOUBLE CROCHET: *Wrap yarn around hook; insert hook through next stitch, wrap yarn around hook and draw through stitch (3 loops on hook). Wrap yarn around hook and draw through all 3 loops on hook.* Repeat between *'s across row or as instructed in specific directions.

FOUNDATION ROW FOR DOUBLE CROCHET: Skip first 2 chains. *Wrap yarn around hook, insert hook in next chain, wrap yarn around hook, draw loop through chain (3 loops on hook); wrap yarn around hook and draw loop through 2 loops and leaving 2 loops on hook. Wrap yarn around hook and draw through the last 2 loops on hook.* Repeat between *'s or as instructed in specific directions.

TREBLE CROCHET: *Wrap yarn around hook twice; insert hook in next stitch; wrap yarn around hook and draw loop through stitch (4 loops on hook); wrap yarn around hook, draw through 2 loops on hook, yarn over hook and again draw through 2 loops on hook, yarn over hook and again draw through 2 loops on hook.* Repeat between *'s across row or as instructed in specific directions.

TO INCREASE: Make 1 stitch as desired, then work a second stitch in the same place, thus adding an extra stitch in a particular row, or as directed.

SINGLE CROCHET DECREASE: Draw a loop through each of 2 stitches; wrap yarn around hook and draw through all 3 loops on hook, thus reducing the number of stitches by one in a particular row, or as directed.

ALL-PURPOSE DECREASE: Work in desired stitch to the particular place in fabric where a decrease is desired. Skip over next stitch without working, then continue across row or as directed, thus reducing the number of stitches by one in a particular row by simply skipping over it.

Crocheted Buttonholes

Work as many rows of single crochet as desired along edge on which the buttonhole band is to be made, or as many as are called for in any specific set of directions. Two or three rows of single crochet are usually worked before the buttonhole rows are done.

On the first buttonhole row, work as follows: Measure buttons to be used to determine their diameter in inches or fractions thereof; determine how many buttons are to be used and where they will be placed. NOTE: Work buttonholes on the right front edge of women's wear and on the left front edge of men's wear.

Mark the place where each buttonhole is to be worked by placing 2 straight pins at these points, leaving a space between each pair of pins that is the exact diameter of the buttons to be used. Work a single crochet in the top of each single crochet made on previous row until a pair of pins is reached; then make a crochet chain the exact length of the space between pins. Single crochet in next stitch directly to the left of second pin and in each stitch thereafter until the next pair of pins is reached. Pins can be removed after each buttonhole chain is worked. Continue this procedure until all buttonholes have been made and end of row has been reached.

On second buttonhole row, work a single crochet in the top of each single crochet made on previous row until a buttonhole is reached. Work as many single crochet stitches through this chain as were skipped on the previous row. For example, if button width (between pins) spanned 3 single crochet stitches, then work 3 single crochet stitches through the buttonhole chain. Continue in this manner until row has been completed, then work as many single crochet rows over the last buttonhole row as desired. Buttonhole band and corresponding button band, which should contain as many rows of single crochet as the buttonhole band, should be at least 1″ in width.

Matching Yarn Buttons

½″ **Diameter:** Using a ✳1 steel hook and ½″ diameter plastic rings, work 14 sc sts through ring. Slip st into first sc worked, then work a sc st in each sc st of first round. Slip st, as in first round. Cut yarn about 12″ from button, draw through loop and pull to tighten. Thread the cut yarn through a yarn needle. Using overcast st, run yarn needle through every other edge st, turn cup-shaped edge downward to back of ring, and pull yarn into a tight closed circle. Fasten securely, insert yarn needle through button base, draw yarn end through and clip close to sts. Sew to garment through this closed-circle shank.

¾″ **Diameter:** Using a ✳00 steel hook and ½″ diameter plastic rings, work 12 sc sts through ring. Slip st into first sc worked, then work 12 sc sts again through ring, over the first round of sts. Slip st, as in first round; cut yarn, draw through loop and pull to tighten. With hook, pull cut end through sts on reverse side and trim close to sts. Sew to garment with matching yarn, inserting yarn needle up through a st at ring center, then down through a st directly opposite. Fasten ends of sewing yarn on reverse side by tying a firm double knot and clipping ends ½″ from fabric.

Part II: EASY ITEMS TO MAKE

SINGLE CROCHET FABRIC

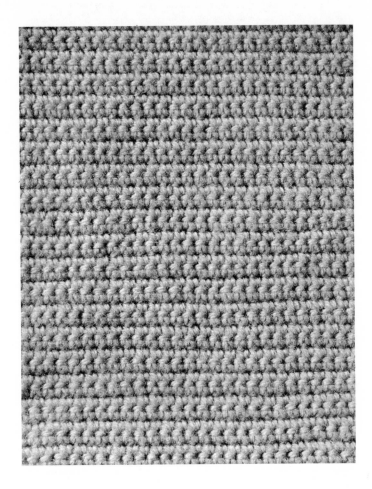

Starting Chain: Any number plus 1 ch for end turn. Sc in 2nd ch from hook and in each ch across row.

Pattern Row: Ch 1, turn work. Sc in each sc across row. Repeat for desired length.

DOUBLE CROCHET FABRIC

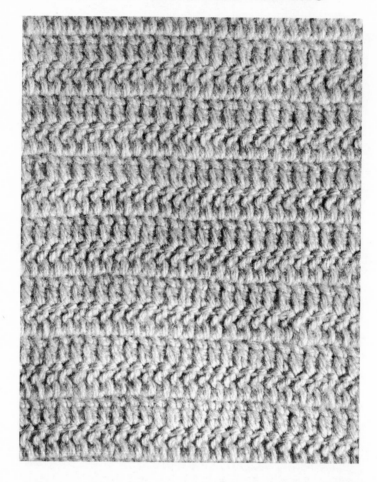

Starting Chain: Any number plus 3 ch for end turn. Dc in 4th ch from hook and in each ch across row.

Pattern Row: Ch 3, turn work. Skip first dc (directly underneath ch 3), dc in each dc across row, dc in top of ch 3 of previous row. Repeat for desired length.

COVERED COAT HANGERS

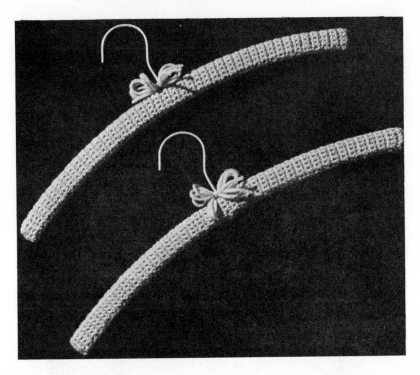

Yarn: Knitting worsted or any yarn of similar weight yielding the proper stitch gauge; 2 oz.

Hook: Steel ⚹0, or any size required to obtain the stitch gauge below.

Stitch Gauge: 5½ sc equal 1″.

Coat Hangers: 2 standard wooden, with metal hooks, as shown.

Apply 3 coats of matching or contrasting color nail polish to metal hooks, allowing each coat to dry thoroughly.

Ch 12, sc in 2nd ch from hook and in each ch across row. Ch 1, turn work, and work in single crochet fabric over these 11 sts until piece measures 14″. Cut yarn and fasten. Fold fabric lengthwise and sew each narrow end together. Fold in half widthwise and determine exact middle of fold. Insert metal hook through fabric at this point. Stretch sewn ends over coat hanger ends. Sew lengthwise edges together. Cut 3 strands of matching yarn, each 10″ long. Place together and tie bow at base of hook, as shown.

SLIPPERS, Square-Toe Style

Yarn: 3-ply bulky, 4 oz for shoe sizes 6 through 7½; 5 oz for sizes 8 and 8½; 6 oz for sizes 9 through 10½; knitting worsted, used double strand throughout, may be substituted.

Hook: Aluminum size G (or any size required to obtain the stitch gauge given below).

Stitch Gauge: 6½ sc equal 2″.

Ch 30 for shoe sizes 6 and 6½
" 32 " " "   7 and 7½
" 34 " " "   8 and 8½
" 36 " " "   9 and 9½
" 38 " " "   10 and 10½

Sc in 2nd ch from hook and in each ch across row to end ch; 3 sc in end ch (heel); turn to opposite side of ch and sc in each ch across row (toe edge); ch 1, turn work to reverse side. Sc in each st across to heel, 3 sc in middle st of the 3 heel sts of previous row, sc in each st around to toe edge. *Ch 1, turn work to reverse side, sc in each st around to corner of straight toe edge.* Repeat between *'s until work measures 7¾" across width of straight toe edge. Cut yarn and fasten.

Assembling and Finishing: Fold corners of slipper at toe edge so that they overlap each other 2½". Pin through all 3 layers of fabric to hold. Sew entire toe edge with overcast st, beginning at one folded edge and ending at the other, making sure that all 3 layers have been sewn together. Turn slipper so that seam is on inside. Crochet a chain 14" long. Pull through upper edges of slipper 3" above toe seam, as shown. Tie a firm single knot in each end of chain and tie in a bow. On second slipper, be sure to reverse the overlapped edges so that it will slant in the opposite direction from first slipper. Before doing this, turn first slipper inside out for comparison.

SLIPPERS, Round-Toe Style

Yarn: 3-ply bulky, 4 oz for shoe sizes 6 through 7½; 5 oz for sizes 8 and 8½; 6 oz for sizes 9 and 9½; knitting worsted, used double strand throughout, may be substituted.

Hook: Aluminum size G (or any size required to obtain the stitch gauge given below).

Stitch Gauge: 6½ sc equal 2″.

Ch 28 for shoe sizes 6 and 6½
″ 30 ″ ″ ″ 7 and 7½
″ 32 ″ ″ ″ 8 and 8½
″ 34 ″ ″ ″ 9 and 9½

Sc in 2nd ch from hook and in each ch across row to end ch; 3 sc in end ch. Turn to opposite side of ch and sc in each ch across row; 3 sc in end st. Continue to work a sc in each st around this oval edge, working 3 sc sts in each curved end of oval 2 more times, then work a sc in each sc around this entire edge until piece measures 2″ from starting ch (double thickness, folded flat). **Shape toe:** Fold slipper flat and place a pin in fabric at fold on one end only. Place a pin at upper edge 2″ from fold on each side of first pin. Decrease over each of these 3 pins by skipping the sc directly above each pin on each round 6 times. Work 1 more round without decreases, ending at fold on opposite end to toe. Slip st in st on fold, cut yarn and fasten.

Bow: Ch 7, sc in 2nd ch from hook and in each ch across row to last ch; 3 sc in end ch. Turn to opposite side of ch and sc in each ch across row; 3 sc in end st. Sc in each st around this oval edge, working 3 sc sts in each curved end of oval 2 more times; end at curved end. Slip st in the next st, cut yarn and fasten. Steam press bow on reverse side. Pinch together, wrap yarn tightly around bow in middle 2 or 3 times and tie securely on reverse side. Sew to toe of slipper, as shown.

SCUFFS

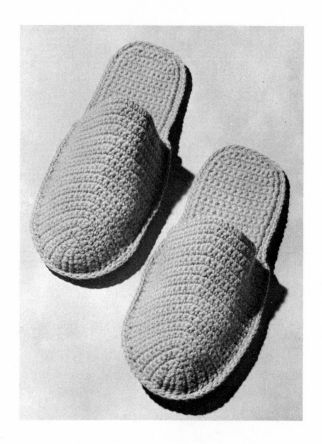

Size: Small (adult shoe size 5½–6), medium (6½–7), large (7½–8).

Yarn: Knitting worsted; 4 oz.

Hook: Small size, use ✂1; medium, use ✂0; large, use ✂0 and ✂00 (✂0 for tops and ✂00 for soles).

Stitch Gauge: Sc on ✂1, 12 sts equal 2″; 14 rows (7 double-row ridges) equal 2″. Sc on ✂0, 11 sts equal 2″; 13 rows (6½ double-row ridges) equal 2″. Sc on ✂00, 10 sts equal 2″; 12 rows (6 double-row ridges) equal 2″.

Additional Materials: Sufficient sheet plastic to make 2 soles. This may be purchased at hobby shops and stationery stores, or large plastic bleach containers may be used by cutting away top and bottom, slitting up 1 side and flattening under heavy book or other weight.

Scuff Tops: Make 2. Beginning at toe, ch 6. Sc in 2nd ch from hook and in each of next 3 ch, 3 sc in end ch, turn ch to opposite edge, 4 sc along ch. *Ch 1, turn work to reverse side sc in each st to curved end, 3 sc in middle st, sc in each st on opposite edge.* Repeat between *'s until there are 21 sts around working edge, then continue as follows: **Rows 1, 2 and 3:** (Ch 1, turn work). Sc in each st around working edge. **Row 4:** (Ch 1, turn work). Sc in each st to middle st at curve 3 sc in middle st, sc in each st along opposite edge. Repeat these 4 rows until a total of 32 rows has been completed (16 double-row ridges), and having 33 sts around working edge. Cut yarn and fasten.

Soles: Make 4. Ch 9, sc in 2nd ch from hook and in each ch across row. (Ch 1, turn work, sc in first st, 2 sc in next st, sc in each st across row to last 2 sts, 2 sc in next st, sc in last st) 2 times (12 sts). *Ch 1, turn work, sc in each st across row.* Repeat between *'s until a total of 24 rows (12 double-row ridges) has been completed from start of work. (Ch 1, turn work, sc in first st, 2 sc in next st, sc in each st across row to last 2 sts, 2 sc in next st, sc in last st) 2 times (16 sts), then repeat between *'s above until a total of 46 rows (23 double-row ridges) has been completed from start of work. (Ch 1, turn work, sc in first st, skip next st, sc in each st across row to last 2 sts, skip next st, sc in last st) 4 times (8 sts remaining and having 50 rows or 25 double-row ridges). Cut yarn and fasten.

Plastic Soles: Make 2. Using a crocheted sole as a pattern, place on plastic, draw around entire edge and cut out.

Assembling and Finishing: Work a row of sc around each separate sole. Place 2 soles together and attach yarn at back of heel. Work a row of sc around edge to center front (toe), making sure both layers of fabric are crocheted together. Slip a plastic sole between layers and continue sc around to starting point. Slip st in first sc to join. Cut yarn and fasten. Make 2nd sole the same. Pin or tack scuff top evenly around front of sole, as shown. Attach yarn at right side of scuff top and work a row of sc around lower edge of scuff top, making sure both top and bottom edges of scuff are crocheted together, and ending at opposite side of scuff top. Cut yarn and fasten.

MEN'S SLIPPERS

Size: Small (shoe size 6–7), medium (8–9), large (10–11).

Yarn: Knitting worsted; 4 oz main color, 2 oz contrasting color.

Hook: For small size, use steel ⚞0; medium, steel ⚞00; large, aluminum or plastic size F (or any sizes required to obtain the stitch gauge given below).

Stitch Gauge: Sc on ⚞0, 5½ sts equal 1″.
                 Sc on ⚞00, 5 sts equal 1″.
                 Sc on size F, 4½ sts equal 1″.

Additional Materials: Slipper tops may be attached to a pair of ready-made soles of proper size if desired.

Slipper Tops: Using main color and beginning at toe, ch 6. Sc in 2nd ch from hook and in each of next 3 ch, 3 sc in end ch, turn ch to opposite edge, 4 sc along ch. *Ch 1, turn work to opposite side, sc in each st to curved end, 3 sc in middle st, sc in each st on opposite edge.* Repeat between *'s until there are 21 sts around working edge, then continue as follows: **Rows 1, 2 and 3:** (Ch 1, turn work), sc in each st around working edge. **Row 4:** (Ch 1, turn work). Sc in each st to middle st at curve, 3 sc in middle st, sc in each st along opposite edge. Repeat these 4 rows until a total of 36 rows has been completed (or 18 double-row ridges), ending on Row 2 and having 35 sts around working edge.

First slipper side: (Ch 1, turn work). Sc across 12 sts. **Next row:** (Ch 1, turn work). Sc in next st, 2 sc in next st, sc in each st across row to outside edge. **Following row:** (Ch 1, turn work). Sc in each st across side-piece row. Repeat these 2 rows until there are 17 sts across side-piece row, then ch 1, turn work, sc in each st across row on each side-piece row until 22 side-piece rows (or 11 double-row ridges) have been completed from start of side piece. Cut yarn and fasten.

Second slipper side: Attach yarn to 12th st from outer edge on opposite side. Ch 1, sc in same st, sc in each st across row to outer edge. **Next row:** (Ch 1, turn work). Sc across to last 2 sts (of side-piece row), 2 sc in next st, sc in last st (of side-piece row). **Following row:** (Ch 1, turn work). Sc in each st across row to outer edge. Repeat these 2 rows until there are 17 sts in row, then complete as for first side piece. Sew these side edges together on what is to be inside of slipper, using overcast st. Attach main color at this seam at upper edge and work a row of sc around entire edge. (On vertical rows, work a sc in edge st of each row, or 2 sc across each double-row ridge.) Slip st in first sc to join. Attach contrasting color and work a sᴄ in each st around to starting point and slip st to join. Work a second contrasting color row the same. Cut yarn and fasten. Attach contrasting color to back seam at lower edge, and work one row of sc around to starting point. Slip st to join. Cut yarn and fasten.

Sole: (Optional; see "Additional Materials" at beginning of directions). Using contrasting color, and beginning at back of heel, ch 11. Sc in 2nd ch from hook and in each ch across row (10 sts). Ch 1, turn work, sc in first st, 2 sc in next st, sc across 6 sts, 2 sc in next st, sc in last st (12 sts). *Ch 1, turn work, sc in each st across row.* Repeat between *'s until 28 rows (14 double-row ridges) have been completed. *Ch 1, turn work, sc in first st, 2 sc in next st, sc in each st across row to last 2 sts, 2 sc in next st, sc in last st. Ch 1, turn work, sc in each st across row.* Work between *'s 2 times (16 sts). *Ch 1, turn work, sc in each st across row.* Repeat between *'s on each row until 48 rows (24 double-row ridges) have been completed from start of work. *Ch 1, turn work, sc in first st, skip next st, sc across row to last 2 sts, skip next st, sc in last st.* Work between *'s 3 times (10 sts remaining). Ch 1, turn work, sc in each st across last row. Work one row of sc around entire outside edge of sole. Slip st to join. Cut yarn and fasten. Pin lower edge of slipper top evenly around outer edge of sole. Using contrasting color and overcast st, sew firmly through both sc edges. Work a row of sc in contrasting color through overcast sts around outer edge, as shown.

GOLD SHOES

Size: Directions are given first for small (shoe size 6–6½); changes for larger sizes (medium, 7–7½, large, 8–8½) follow in parentheses.

Yarn: Metallic yarn, gold or silver; 3 125-yard balls; bedspread crochet cotton (for soles), 3 200-yard balls.

Hook: Steel ⚹00 for metallic yarn; ⚹0 for bedspread cotton (or any sizes required to obtain the stitch gauge given below).

Stitch Gauge: Metallic yarn is worked double strand and the bedspread cotton is worked triple strand throughout (except where noted for sewing seams). Metallic yarn, 10 sc equal 2″, 10 rows equal 2″. Bedspread cotton, 12 sc equal 2″, 12 rows equal 2″.

Additional Materials: Plastic for upper sole; white fabric glue; round elastic.

Shoe Tops: Using metallic yarn double strand and ⚹00 hook, ch 5, sc in 2nd ch from hook and in next 2 ch, 3 sc in end ch, 3 sc in next 3 ch on opposite side. Ch 1, turn work, sc in each st to middle st, 3 sc in middle st, sc in each st around opposite edge. *Ch 1, turn work, sc in each st around entire working edge, ch 1, turn work, sc in each st to middle st, 3 sc in middle st, sc in each st around to opposite edge.* Repeat between *'s until 20 (21, 21) rows have been completed and have 29 sts across working edge. (Each ridge in fabric represents 2 rows.)

First side piece: *Ch 1, turn work, sc in each of next 7 sts.* Repeat between *'s for 10 rows, then work increase row: Sc in first st, 2 sc in next st, sc in each st across row. Continue repeating between *'s (as before) until 20 rows have been completed, work another increase row, then continue between *'s until 29 (30, 32) side-piece rows have been completed. Cut yarn and fasten.

Opposite side piece: Attach yarn at 7th st from edge on opposite side, ch 1, sc in each st across these 7 sts, then work between *'s as for first side piece for 10 rows.

Increase Row: Ch 1, turn work; sc across row to last 2 sts; 2 sc in next st, sc in last st. Continue working between *'s until 20 rows have been completed, work another increase row, then complete as for first side piece. Sew side-piece edges together on what is to be the inside, using yarn single strand and overcast st. Attach yarn to back of heel at lower edge and work 1 row sc around entire lower edge, slip st to first st to join.

Sole: Using cotton yarn triple strand and ⚹0 hook, ch 7, sc in 2nd ch from hook and in each ch across row. (Ch 1, turn work. Sc in first st, 2 sc in next st, sc across row to last 2 sts, 2 sc in next st, sc in last st) 3 times. *Ch 1, turn work, sc in each st across row.* Repeat between *'s until 14 (16, 18) rows have been completed from start. (Ch 1, turn work, sc in each st across row. Ch 1, turn work, sc in first st, skip next st, sc in each remaining st across row) 2 times, then continue working between *'s (as before) until 26 (28, 30) rows have been completed from start. **Next row:** Ch 1, turn work, sc in first st, 2 sc in next st, sc in each st across row to last 2 sts, 2 sc in next st, sc in last st. (Ch 1, turn work, sc in first st. 2 sc in next st— this increase made on same edge as skipped st decreases were made—sc in each remaining st across row. Ch 1, turn work, sc in each st across row) 6 times, to total 18 sts across row, then continue working between *'s (as before) until 44 (46, 48) rows have been completed from start. **Decrease row:** Ch 1, turn work, sc in first st, skip next st, sc in each st across row to last 2 sts, skip next st, sc in last st. **Next 3 rows:** Ch 1, turn work, sc in each st across row. Repeat these last 4 rows until 54 (58, 60) rows have been completed from start, then work decrease row (only) for 3 (4, 3) more rows. Cut yarn and fasten. Steam press soles.

Plastic Sole: Lay crocheted sole on flat plastic and draw around. Cut out 2 plastic soles. Attach yarn to back of crocheted sole and work 1 row sc around entire outside edge. Slip st to join. Lay crocheted soles on flat surface, turning so that one is for left foot and one is for right foot. Spread a thin coating of fabric glue over surface of plastic soles and press onto crocheted soles, centering properly. Cover with plastic wrap or foil and press flat with heavy books or other weights until glue is thoroughly dry. Pin or tack lower edge of slipper top evenly around sc edge of sole, plastic side up, matching heel and toe of top to heel and toe of sole. Using metallic yarn single strand, attach to back of heel and sew sc edge of top to sc edge of lower sole, using overcast st, then sew a second time, using overcast st and metallic yarn double strand.

Elastic Top: Thread round elastic through yarn needle and fasten end of elastic to angle made by first row of side piece. Run elastic in and out of upper edge of slipper to side piece angle on opposite side. Fasten securely. Using metallic yarn double strand, work a row of sc at upper edge over elastic. A cushion innersole of proper size may be inserted over plastic sole.

SCATTER RUG

Size: Approximately 20″×28″, exclusive of fringe.

Yarn: Bulky wool yarn or any material yielding the stitch gauge given below; 16 oz main color and 1 oz contrasting color.

Hook: Aluminum size G (or any size required to obtain the stitch gauge given below).

Stitch Gauge: 3 sc equal 1″.

Using main color, ch 53 and work in single crochet fabric (making sure there are 52 sts in each row) until rug measures 28″ long. Cut yarn and fasten. Work 1 row sc along each long edge of rug.

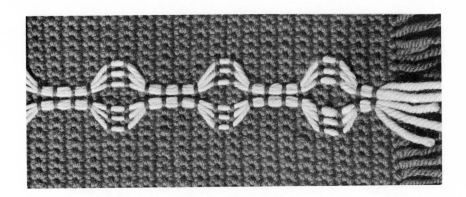

Surface Weave Motif: Using contrasting color and large yarn needle, weave pattern through stitch strands across length of rug, as shown, leaving 3″ strands at beginning and end of each weaving row.

Fringe: Using main color, cut strands 6″ long. Fold a strand in half. With hook, pull through edge st on reverse side to form a loop about ¾″ long. Pull cut ends through this loop and pull to tighten. Repeat on each st across each short edge, skipping sts where contrasting color forms fringe, as shown. Trim edges of fringe even where necessary.

ADJUSTABLE BELT

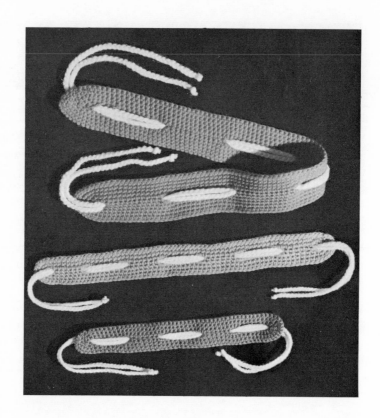

Yarn: Knitting worsted; 2 oz dark color, 1 oz light color.

Hook: Steel ╳00 (or any size required to obtain the stitch gauge given below).

Stitch Gauge: 5 sc equal 1″.

Using dark color, ch 117; sc in 5th ch from hook and in next 13 ch, *ch 2, skip 2 ch, sc in next 14 ch.* Repeat between *'s across ch, ending: Ch 2, skip 2 ch, sc in last ch.

Round 1: Turn to opposite side of ch, 3 sc through first 2 ch, *sc in each of next 14 sts, 3 sc through ch-2 space.* Repeat between *'s across row, ending: Sc in each of next 14 ch, 6 sc in ch-4 end loop, then continue between *'s across opposite side, ending: 3 sc through end loop. Sc in each sc across row, 2 sc in each of 4 end sts, sc in each st across opposite side, 2 sc in each of 4 sts on opposite end. Continue working in this manner on each round until belt measures 2" wide. **Tie:** Using light color double strand, make 2 chs, each about 40" long. Steam press belt on reverse side and allow to dry flat. Run chs in and out of eyelets, as shown. Tie a single knot in each end of each ch.

ADJUSTABLE HEADBAND

Yarn: Knitting worsted; 1 oz dark color, ½ oz light color.

Hook and Stitch Gauge: Same as for adjustable belt.

Using dark color, ch 62, sc in 5th ch from hook and in each of next 5 ch, *ch 2, skip 2 ch, sc in next 6 ch.* Repeat between *'s across ch, ending: Ch 2, skip 2 ch, sc in last ch.
Round 1: Turn to opposite side of ch, 3 sc through first 2 ch, *sc in each of next 6 sts, 3 sc through ch-2 space.* Repeat between *'s across row, ending: Sc in each of next 6 ch, 6 sc in ch-4 end loop, then repeat between *'s across opposite side, ending: Sc in each of next 6 sts, 3 sc through end loop. Sc in each sc across row, 2 sc in each of 4 end sts, sc in each sc across opposite side, 2 sc in each of 4 sts on opposite end. Work one more round, working 2 sc in each of 4 end sts on each curved end. Slip st in next st, cut yarn and fasten.

Ties: Using light color, make 2 ch each about 26" long. Run in and out of eyelets, as shown. Tie a single knot in each end of each ch.

ADJUSTABLE DOG COLLAR

Yarn, Hook and Stitch Gauge: Same as for adjustable headband.

Using dark color, ch 46, then work the same as for adjustable headband. Using light color, make 2 chs about 22" long, or desired length to fit neck of individual animal. Finish as for headband.

ANKLE BOOTEES AND CAP

Size: Directions are given first for infant size; changes for 3–6 months' size follow in parentheses.

Yarn: 5 oz knitting worsted.

Hook: Steel ✕00 (or any size required to obtain the stitch gauge given below).

Stitch Gauge: 5 sc equal 1″.

Bootees: Ch 16 (20); sc is 2nd ch from hook and in each ch across row; 3 sc in end ch, turn ch and work a sc in each ch on opposite side; 3 sc in end ch. Continue working a sc in each sc around, working 3 sc in each end 2 more times, then work a sc in each sc around until bootee measures 1½″ from starting ch (double thickness, folded flat). **Shape toe:** Sc around to beginning of curve on opposite side, skip 1 sc (a decrease), sc in next sc, work to end st (at fold), skip a sc, sc in next st, work to opposite curve to correspond with first decrease, skip 1 sc, sc in next st, work around to opposite side (heel). Repeat these 3 skipped-st decreases on same side 3 (4) more times; work to back of heel. Slip st, ch 3, skip a sc, *hdc in next sc, ch 1.* Repeat between *'s around to starting point, slip st in 2nd ch of ch 3. **Next round:** Ch 1, sc through each ch 1 and in top of each hdc around to starting point. Slip st to join. **Edging:** Ch 3, 2 dc at base of ch 3, skip 2 sc, *sc in next st, ch 2, 2 dc in same space, skip 2 sc.* Repeat between *'s around to starting point. Slip st in last st. Cut yarn and fasten. **Tie:** Make a ch 15″ long. Run in and out of hdc at ankle. Tie a single knot in each end and tie bow over toe section, as shown.

Cap: Ch 30 (33), sc in 2nd ch from hook and in each ch across row; 2 sc in end ch, turn ch and sc in each ch on opposite side. *Ch 1, turn work and sc in each st across one side, around curved edge, and across opposite side to straight edge.* Repeat between *'s until cap measures 5¼″ (5¾″). **Edging:** Work edging on last row as for bootees. **Lower edge:** Ch 3, turn corner, hdc at edge of first row, then (ch 1, hdc) in edge st of every other row around to opposite side, ch 3, slip st into first st of edging.

Tie: Make a ch about 28″ long. Run in and out of hdc at lower edge of cap. Tie a single knot in each end.

HEXAGON POT HOLDER

Yarn: Heavy rug cotton or bulky acrylic yarn; 1 skein.

Hook: Aluminum size G.

Make 2 of the following: Ch 5, slip st to form ring. Ch 3, 2 dc in ring. (Ch 1, 3 dc in ring) 5 times, ch 1, slip st in top of ch 3 to join.

Pattern Round: Ch 3, *dc in top of each dc to ch 1, dc, ch 1, dc in ch 1.* Repeat between *'s around to last ch 1 and end: Dc in top of each dc to ch 3, slip st in top of ch 3 to join. Repeat pattern round until 5 rounds have been completed from start. Cut yarn and fasten. With reverse sides together, attach yarn through both layers of pot holder at a ch 1 space. Crochet these 2 pieces together with 1 row of sc, working 2 sc in each ch 1 space, around to starting point. Ch 6 for hanging loop, slip st into first sc made. Cut yarn and fasten. Tack pot holder pieces together at center.

GOLF CLUB COVERS

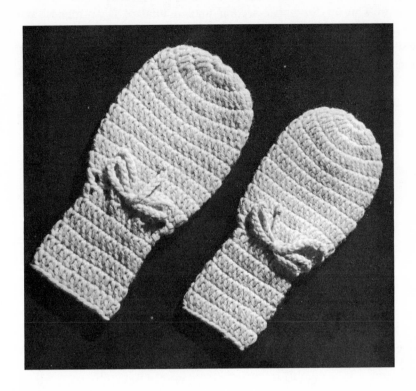

Size: Directions are given first for irons. Changes for woods follow in parentheses.

Yarn: Knitting worsted; 1 oz for each cover.

Hook: Use plastic or aluminum size F for woods and steel ⚡0 for irons.

Stitch Gauge: 8 dc equal 2″ on size F hook; 10 dc equal 2″ on ⚡0 hook.

Ch 4, slip st in first ch to form ring. Ch 1, 12 sc through ring. Slip st into first sc, ch 3, dc in base of ch 3, 2 dc in each sc around to starting point, totaling 23 dc plus ch 3. Slip st in top of ch 3 to join. **Next round:** Ch 3, *dc in top of next dc, 2 dc in top of next dc.* Repeat between *'s around to starting point, dc in last dc. Slip st in top of ch 3 to join. *Ch 3, work a dc in top of each dc around to starting point, slip st into top of ch 3 to join.* Repeat between *'s until a total of 10 dc rounds has been completed.

Filet round for tie: Ch 3, dc in top of next dc, ch 1, skip next dc, *dc in top of each of next 2 dc, ch 1, skip next dc.* Repeat between *'s around to starting point, slip st into top of ch 3 to join. Ch 3, dc in top of each dc around (skipping over each ch 1) to starting point. Slip stitch to join. Continue working as for upper section until a total of 6 dc rounds has been completed below filet round. Cut yarn and fasten. **Tie:** Make a ch about 16″ long. Run in and out of ch-1 filet openings. Tie a single knot in each end of ch at desired length and trim off excess.

WALKING COAT FOR DOG OR CAT

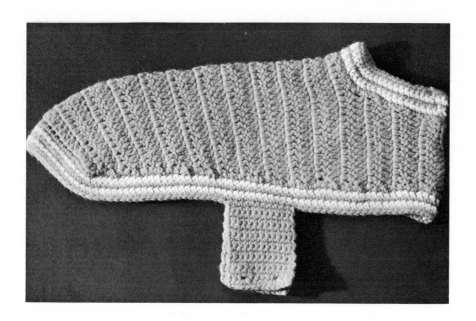

Size: Directions are given first for small dog or cat. Changes for medium-size dog or medium-to-large cat follow in parentheses.

Yarn: Knitting worsted; 1 4-oz skein, plus about 6 yards of contrasting color for trim.

Hook: Steel ✳00 (or any size required to obtain the stitch gauge given below).

Stitch Gauge: 8 double crochet stitches equal 2″.

Buttons: 2, ½″ to ⅝″ diameter; flat.

Ch 26 (33); dc in 4th ch from hook and in each ch across row. **Row 1:** Ch 3 (count as dc), turn work, 2 dc in top of next dc (an increase), dc in top of each dc across row to last dc, 2 dc in top of last dc. **Row 2:** Ch 3, turn work, dc in top of each dc across row. Repeat Rows 1 and 2 until there are 42 (47) dc across row, then repeat Row 2 only until coat measures 1″ less than length of back of animal (when measured from base of tail to base of neck).

Shape neck: Working each shoulder separately, ch 3 (count as dc), turn and work 16 (18) dc, *ch 3 (count as dc), turn, skip first dc (a decrease), dc in top of each dc across row.* Repeat between *'s until 12 (14) sts remain, then repeat Row 2 until shoulder measures 3″ (4″). Beginning at outside edge, work last row: Ch 3, work 4 dc, 4 hdc, 3 (5) sc across row. Cut yarn and fasten. Attach yarn to outer edge of opposite side and work corresponding shoulder the same.

Assembling and Finishing: Sew center front seam. Work 3 rounds of sc around neckline and entire outer edge of coat, alternating main color and contrasting color, as shown. **Buttonhole tab:** Using 2 pins, mark a 2″ space in exact middle of lower edge on one side. Join yarn at right pin and work a sc in each of next 12 sc. Remove pins and *ch 1, turn work, sc across 12 sts.* Repeat between *'s across each row until tab measures 2½″ (3½″). **Next row:** Ch 1, turn work, sc in each of next 2 sc, ch 2, skip 2 sc, sc in each of next 4 sts, ch 2, skip 2, sc in each of last 2 sc, ch 1, turn work. **Last row:** Sc across row, working 2 sc in each ch 2 of previous row. Cut yarn and fasten. **Button tab:** In the same position on opposite side, work as for buttonhole tab, omitting buttonhole rows and working until tab measures 3″ (4″) from start. Sew buttons to tab to correspond with buttonholes, adjusting placement of buttons from edge of tab to fit individual animal. Block to desired measurements.

TAM

Size: Fits all teen-age and adult head sizes.

Yarn: Knitting worsted; 4 oz.

Hook: ✳00 for average tension; for tighter tension, use 1 size larger hook.

Tam is made in one piece, beginning at center top. Ch 6, join with slip st to form ring. **Round 1:** Ch 3, 17 dc in ring, join with slip st to top of ch 3. **Round 2:** Ch 3, 2 dc in each st of previous round. Slip st to join. **Round 3:** Ch 3, *2 dc in next st, dc in next st.* Repeat between *'s around and end: 2 dc in last st. Slip st to join. **Round 4:** Ch 3, *dc in each of next 2 sts, 2 dc in next st.* Repeat between *'s around and end: Dc in each of last 2 sts, dc in same space as ch 3; slip st to join. **Round 5:** Ch 3, *dc in each of next 6 sts, 2 dc in next st.* Repeat between *'s around, ending last repeat (if less than 7 sts); dc in each st to ch 3, dc in same space as ch 3, slip st to join. Repeat Round 5 until a total of 10 rounds has been completed from start (round 1). **Brimline turn round:** Ch 1, turn to reverse side and work 1 sc in each st around to starting point. Slip st to join. Turn work to right side. (Work a decrease as follows: Yarn over hook, draw a loop through next st, draw a loop through 2 loops on hook, yarn over hook, draw a loop through next st, draw a loop through 2 loops on hook, then draw yarn through all loops on hook.) **Decrease round:** *Ch 3, work a decrease in next 2 sts, dc in each of next 6 sts.* Repeat between *'s around to starting point, ending last repeat (if less than 8 sts): Dc in each st to ch 3. Slip st to join. Repeat decrease round until a total of 5 decrease rounds has been completed, making a total of 15 dc rounds from start (round 1). Work 2 rows sc around edge, slip st to join. Cut yarn and fasten. If a smaller head size is desired, work another sc round, skipping 1 st every 4 or 5 sts at even intervals around to starting point. Steam press lightly on reverse side, or block to desired size. Make a large pompon and sew securely to center top, as shown.

TOTE BAG

Size: Approximately 14″ square.

Yarn: Knitting worsted; 2 4-oz skeins main color for bag; about 1 oz flower color A and about ½ oz flower color B.

Hook: Aluminum size G for bag and steel ╳0 for flower trim.

Buttons: 2, 1″ to 1¼″ diameter.

Using main color yarn double strand and size G hook, ch 45; sc in 2nd ch from hook and in each ch across row, 3 sc in end ch. Turn to opposite side of ch and work a sc in each corresponding ch; work 3 sc in end ch. *Ch 3, work a dc in each st around this circular edge, slip st in top of ch 3 to join.* Repeat between *'s until bag measures 13½" from start, making sure that each round contains exactly the same number of dc. Work 1 round of sc at upper edge, slip st to join. Cut yarn and fasten. **Handle:** Using main color double strand and size G hook, ch 122. Sc in 2nd ch from hook and in each ch across row; 3 sc in end ch, turn and work a sc in each ch across opposite side and 3 sc in end ch. Slip st in first sc made. Cut yarn and fasten. Block pieces. Sew each end of handle to sides of bag, as shown.

Flower Trim: (Make 2.) Using ⚹0 hook and color A single strand, ch 12, slip st to form ring; ch 1, 24 sc in ring, slip st in ch 1, *4 sc in each of 4 sc of previous row, ch 1, turn.* Repeat between *'s until 6 rows have been completed. **Next row:** Draw a loop through each of the 4 sc (5 loops on hook), draw yarn through all loops on hook, ch 1. Cut yarn and fasten (a petal made). Attach yarn to base of petal on left side and work another petal. Repeat until a total of 6 petals has been made. Attach matching yarn between 2 petals and work a row of sc around each petal, working 3 sc in tip of each petal and a slip st at base of each petal. Fasten with a slip st. Cut yarn and fasten. Using color B, work 1 more row sc around each petal, as before. Slip st and fasten.

Bow and Stems: Using color A double strand and size G hook, crochet a ch about 32" long. Tie a bowknot in middle of ch to form loops about 3" long. Arrange on bag, as shown, and tack firmly to bag at knot, at ends of loops and along stems at 1" intervals, using a half strand of matching yarn. Sew flowers and button centers firmly to bag at ends of ch, as shown.

CAPELET

Yarn: Baby wool; 10 oz.

Hook: Plastic or metal size F (or any size required to obtain the stitch gauge below).

Stitch Gauge: 10 dc equal 2″.

Beginning at neckline, ch 91. Sc in 2nd ch from hook and in each ch across row. Ch 3, turn work.

Starting Row: Skip first sc, dc in each of next 4 sc, *ch 1, skip next 2 sc; in next sc work 2 dc, ch 2, 2 dc (a shell made); ch 1, skip next 2 sc, dc in each of next 10 sc.* Repeat between *'s across row, ending last repeat: Dc in last 5 sc. Ch 3, turn work.

Pattern Row: Skip first dc, dc in each dc across to first ch 1, *dc through next ch 1; ch 1, shell through ch-2 space of next shell, ch 1, dc through next ch 1, dc in each dc across to next ch 1.* Repeat between *'s across row, ending last repeat: Dc in each dc across to ch 3, dc in top of ch 3. Ch 3, turn work.

Repeat pattern row until work measures 17½″ from start, measured between shell patterns. Cut yarn and fasten.

Edging: Attach yarn at lower right center front edge and work a row of sc up right edge, working 2 sc in each ch-3 or dc space to neck edge. On neck edge, work a sc in each ch across row. Work down left center front edge to correspond with right edge. Work shell edging along lower edge as follows: Skip first 2 dc, *2 dc, ch 2, 2 dc in next st, skip 2 sts, dc in next dc, skip 2 sts.* Repeat between *'s across to last 3 or 4 sts and end: Skip 2 sts, 2 dc, ch 2, 2 dc in next to last st, sc in last st. Cut yarn and fasten.

Neckline: With inside of capelet turned out, attach yarn at right edge of neckline, ch 3 and work a dc in each sc across neckline edge. Ch 1, turn, then work a row of shell edging the same as for lower edge. Cut yarn and fasten.

Chain Tie: Using yarn double strand, make a ch about 44″ long. Weave in and out of each 2 dc under shell edging at neckline. Attach pompons at ends of ch, if desired. Block or steam press lightly on reverse side.

CARDIGAN CAPELET

Size: This loose-fitting garment will accommodate bust sizes 34″ through 44″.

Yarn: Knitting worsted; 20 oz.

Hook: Aluminum size G (or any size required to obtain the stitch gauge given below).

Stitch Gauge: 4 dc equal 1″.

Beginning at neckline, ch 89, making sure that ch is neither too tight nor too loose.

Starting Row: Dc in 4th ch from hook and in each ch across row, ch 3, turn work.

Panel Row 1: Skip first 2 dc, *dc in each of next 2 dc, 3 dc in next dc, dc in each of next 2 dc (a pattern panel made); skip next dc.* Repeat between *'s across row and end: Dc in top of ch. Ch 3, turn work.

Panel Row 2: Skip first 2 dc, *dc in each of next 2 dc, 5 dc in next dc, dc in each of next 2 dc, skip next 2 dc.* Repeat between *'s across row, skip last dc, dc in top of ch 3. Ch 3, turn work.

Panel Row 3: Skip first 2 dc, *dc in each dc to middle dc of next pattern panel, 3 dc in middle dc, dc in each dc to (but not including) last dc of pattern panel, skip next 2 dc.* Repeat between *'s across row, skip last dc, dc in top of ch 3. Ch 3, turn work.

Panel Row 4: Skip first 2 dc, *dc in each dc to middle dc of next pattern panel, 5 dc in middle dc, dc in each dc to (but not including) last dc of pattern panel, skip next 2 dc.* Repeat between *'s across row, skip last dc, dc in top of ch 3. Ch 3, turn work.

Repeat panel rows 3 and 4 until 23 rows have been completed from start, ending on row 4.

Arm Openings: Skip first 2 dc, dc in top of each dc across to middle dc of next pattern panel, 3 dc in middle dc, dc in each dc to within last dc of pattern panel, skip next 2 dc, dc in each dc across to middle dc of next pattern panel, 3 dc in middle dc, dc across to last dc of pattern panel; skip next 3 pattern panels and first dc of next pattern panel, dc in next dc (sleeve opening made). Work across next 4 pattern panels, skip next 3 pattern panels and first dc of next pattern panel, work across last 2 pattern panels to last dc, dc in top of ch 3. Ch 3, turn work. Work panel row 4 across body of capelet below sleeve openings, then repeat panel rows 3 and 4 three more times to total 16 rows below sleeve openings. Cut yarn and fasten. **Sleeves:** With reverse side of 23rd row facing, attach yarn to middle of underarm and work 4 rows, as follows: **Row 1:** Ch 3, dc in base of next dc, skip next 2 dc, dc in next dc, work in pattern around sleeve to last dc of pattern panel, dc at base of next dc at underarm. Slip st in top of ch 3. Ch 3, turn work. **Row 2:** Skip 2 dc, dc in next dc, work in pattern around sleeve to last dc on last pattern panel. Slip st in top of ch 3. Ch 3, turn work. **Rows 3 and 4:** Skip next dc, dc in next dc, work in pattern around to last dc of pattern panel. Slip st in top of ch 3. Cut yarn and fasten. **Edging:** Attach yarn at lower right center front edge and work a row of sc up right edge, working 2 sc in each ch 3 or dc space to neck edge. On neck edge, work a sc through starting ch between each dc. Work down left center front edge to correspond with right edge. Cut yarn and fasten. NOTE: If longer garment or longer sleeves are desired, work 2 or 3 additional pattern rows, or attach 3″ or 4″ fringe around sleeves and lower edges. **Tie:** Using yarn double strand, crochet a ch about 36″ long. Run in and out of dc at neckline. Attach pompons to ends of chain tie, if desired.

Part III: A COLLECTION OF
PATTERN STITCHES
Easy-Shape Items to Make

SOLID SHELL

Suggested Uses: Cardigans, pullovers, baby wear, hats, bags, vests, coverlets, place setting mats, ornamental cuffs, collars, pockets.

Starting Chain: Multiple of 6 plus 1. Sc in 2nd ch from hook and in each ch across row. Ch 1, turn work.

Starting Row: *Skip 2 sc, 5 dc in next sc; skip 2 sc, sc in next sc.* Repeat between *'s across row. Ch 3, turn work.

Row 1: 2 dc in sc (at base of ch 3), *skip 2 dc, sc in next dc, skip 2 dc, 5 dc in next sc.* Repeat between *'s across row and end: Skip 2 dc, sc in next dc, skip 2 dc, 3 dc in ch 1 of previous row. Ch 1, turn work.

Row 2: *5 dc in next sc, skip 2 dc, sc in next dc.* Repeat between *'s across row and end last repeat: Sc in top of ch 3 of previous row. Ch 3, turn work.

Repeat Rows 1 and 2 for pattern. For 2-color pattern, as shown, use color A for starting ch and starting row, then alternate color B on Row 1 and Color A on Row 2.

CARDIGAN in Solid Shell Pattern

Size: Directions are given first for small (bust size 34″ through 36″); changes for medium (38″ through 40″) follow in parentheses.

Yarn: Knitting worsted; 28 oz.

Hook: Small size, use plastic or aluminum size F; medium, size G (or any size required to obtain the stitch gauge given below).

Stitch Gauge: Size F, 2 shell patterns and 2 sc sts equal 3¼″; size G, 3½″.

Buttons: ¾″ diameter, 4.

Back: Ch 85 loosely and work in Solid Shell pattern until piece measures 16" from start (or desired length from lower edge to underarm), ending on pattern row 1. Cut yarn and fasten. Sleeve inset: Turn work and attach yarn to middle of 2nd full shell from right edge. Work pattern row 2 across to last 2 full shells at left edge and end row in middle of 2nd full shell from left. Ch 1, turn work and continue in pattern until sleeve insets measure 7½" (8"), ending on a pattern row 1. Cut yarn and fasten.

Right and Left Fronts: Ch 43 loosely and work in pattern until piece measures 16" from start (or desired length to match back), ending on pattern row 1. On next row, work across to middle of 2nd full shell from left edge. Ch 1, turn work and continue in pattern until sleeve inset measures the same as for back, ending on a pattern row 1. Cut yarn and fasten.

Sleeves: Ch 43; sc in 2nd ch from hook and in each ch across row. *Ch 1, turn work, sc in each sc across row.* Repeat between *'s on each row until piece measures 1", then work in pattern until work measures approximately 4½" from start, ending on pattern row 2. Ch 3, turn work. **Increase on next row 1 as follows:** 4 dc in first sc (at base of ch 3), work in pattern across row and end: 5 dc in last sc. Ch 3, turn work. **Next row:** 2 dc at base of ch 3, sc in middle of first shell and work in pattern row 1 across, then continue in pattern, working increase rows (as above) when work measures approximately 9", 12" and 14" from start (to total 4 increases). Continue in pattern until sleeve measures 18" from start (or desired length when measured from shoulder edge to wrist). Cut yarn and fasten.

Collar: Sew shoulder seams, using overcast st, from outer edges to middle of 3rd full shell, leaving 3 full shells and 2 half shells for back neckline and 1 full shell and 2 half shells each side of front neckline for lapels, on what is to be the reverse side of work. (See photo.) With right side facing, attach yarn to upper corner of right edge and work across to upper left corner in pattern. Repeat pattern until a total of 8 rows has been completed. Cut yarn and fasten.

Assembling: Pin upper horizontal edge of sleeve along vertical edge of sleeve inset and sew on reverse side, using overcast st. Sew upper vertical edges of sleeve to horizontal edges of sleeve inset. Sew balance of vertical sleeve seams together to lower edge. Sew side seams.

Finishing: With right side facing, attach yarn to lower corner of right center front and work in sc, catching 2 outer edge strands on each sc along this edge, around edge of collar, working 3 sts in each corner, and down left center front edge. Ch 1, turn, sc in each sc of previous row and working 3 sts in each corner st of collar, to lower right edge (starting point). **Buttonhole row:** Ch 1, turn work to right side; sc in next 15 sc of previous row; (ch 3, skip 3 sc, sc in next 12 sc) 4 times, then work a sc in each sc of previous row, working 3 sc in each corner of collar. **Next row:** Ch 1, turn work. Sc in each sc around to right center front edge, working 3 sc in each corner of collar, then work a sc in each sc and 3 sc through each ch 3 (buttonhole made) to starting point. **Last row:** Ch 1, turn work. Sc in each sc up right center front, 3 sc in each corner of collar, down left center front edge, 3 sc in corner; then work 1 row of sc around entire lower edge of cardigan, working 3 sc to turn corner. Slip st into sc at starting point (lower corner of right center front). Cut yarn and fasten. Block to desired measurements. Sew buttons to left edge to correspond with buttonholes.

LACY SHELL

Suggested Uses: Afghans, coverlets, baby wear, dresses, blouses, stoles, mufflers, cardigans, women's vests, place setting mats, tablecloths.

Starting Chain: Multiple of 6 plus 3. Sc in 2nd ch from hook and in each ch across row. Ch 3, turn work, skip 3 sc, 3 dc in next sc, ch 2, 3 dc in same sc (a shell made). *Skip 5 sc, work a shell in next sc.* Repeat between *'s across row and end: Skip 3 sc, dc in last sc. Ch 3, turn work.
Pattern Row: *Work a shell through ch 2 of next shell.* Repeat between *'s across row and end: Dc in top of ch 3. Ch 3, turn work.
Repeat pattern row for desired length.

WOMEN'S VEST in Lacy Shell

(Not illustrated)

Size: Directions are given first for small (32"–34" bust). Changes for larger sizes (medium, 36"–38"; large, 40"–42"; generous large, 44"–46") follow in parentheses.

Yarn: Knitting worsted; 12 oz.

Hook: Aluminum size G (or any size required to obtain the stitch gauge given below).

Stitch Gauge: 2 shells equal 3"; 2 rows equal 1½".

Back: Beginning at lower edge, ch 75 (81, 87, 93) and work in Lacy Shell pattern until a total of 22 shell rows has been completed. Cut yarn and fasten. Arm openings: Turn work to opposite side and attach yarn between 2nd and 3rd shell at upper right edge. Ch 3, work in pattern across row to last 2 shells; dc in space between 2nd and 3rd shells from left edge. Ch 3, turn work and continue in shell pattern over these 8 (9, 10, 11) shells until a total of 12 (12, 13, 14) shell rows has been completed. Cut yarn and fasten.

Fronts: Ch 39 (39, 45, 45) and work until a total of 22 shell rows has been completed. **Arm opening:** Work across next row to last 2 shells, dc in space between 2nd and 3rd shell from left edge, ch 3, turn work. Continue in pattern until 3 (3, 4, 4) shell rows have been completed. **Neckline:** Work across next row to last 2 shells, dc in space between 2nd and 3rd shell from edge on opposite side from arm opening, ch 3, turn work. Continue in pattern until a total of 12 (12, 13, 14) shell rows has been completed above arm opening. Cut yarn and fasten. Sew shoulder and side seams on reverse side, using overcast st.

Chain Ties: Attach yarn to front neckline edge and work a chain about 15" long. Repeat on opposite side. Pompons may be attached to ends of chains, if desired. Block to desired measurements.

LATTICE SHELL

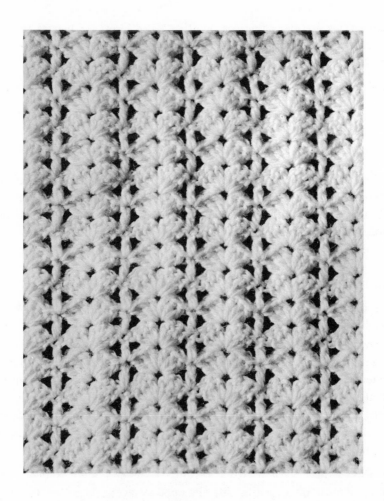

Suggested Uses: Dresses, blouses, baby wear, place setting mats, mufflers, stoles, bedspreads.

Starting Chain: Multiple of 6 plus 1. Sc in 2nd ch from hook and in each ch across row. Ch 3, turn work.

Starting Row: *Skip 2 sc, 3 dc in next sc, ch 2, 3 dc in same sc (a shell made), skip 2 sc, dc in next sc.* Repeat between *'s across row. Ch 3, turn work.

Pattern Row: *Work a shell through ch-2 space of next shell, dc in top of dc between shells.* Repeat between *'s across row and end: Dc in top of ch 3. Ch 3, turn work.

Repeat pattern row for desired length.

BLOUSE in Lattice Shell Pattern

Size: Directions are given first for bust size 32″–34″. Changes for larger sizes (36″–38″, 40″–42″, 44″–46″) follow in parentheses.

Yarn: Use any lightweight sports or dress yarn yielding the stitch gauge given below. Sizes 32 through 38, 14 oz; larger sizes, 18 oz. (If a shorter length is desired, less yarn may be required; if a longer length is desired, more yarn may be required.)

Hook: Steel ✕00 (or any size required to obtain the stitch gauge given below).

Stitch Gauge: 3 shell patterns equal 3½″; 2 rows equal 1″.

Back: Beginning at upper edge, ch 121 (133, 145, 157) and work in Lattice Shell pattern for 6½" (7", 7½", 8"). Cut yarn and fasten. (Sleeve section completed.) Turn work and attach yarn to dc following 3rd shell from right edge. Ch 3 and work in pattern across row to dc preceding 3rd shell from left edge. Ch 3, turn work. Continue in pattern over middle shells until work measures 22" (23", 23", 24") or desired length from start. Cut yarn and fasten.

Fronts: Make 2 of the following (sleeve section and neckline opening). Ch 61 (67, 73, 79) and work in pattern for 6½" (7", 7½", 8"). Cut yarn and fasten. Complete 2nd front section and turn both pieces so that the reverse side of last pattern row is facing; place side by side with starting ch at lower edge. Attach yarn to dc following 3rd shell from right edge (as for middle section of back). Work in pattern across first piece to opposite edge; continue across 2nd piece, skipping the first dc (and connecting it to first piece) to dc preceding 3rd shell from left edge. Ch 3, turn work and finish as for back, making sure that front contains the same number of pattern rows as are in back.

Collar: Sew upper sleeve and shoulder seams on reverse side, leaving a 7" opening in middle for neckline (3½" opening on each side of front neckline separation). Turn to right side and fold lapels back on each side. Attach yarn at upper corner of lapel on right-hand side. Ch 3, then work starting row of Lattice Shell pattern between *'s across right lapel, back of neckline and left lapel, working a shell in base of each shell and a dc in base of each dc across row. Ch 3, turn work, then work pattern row until collar measures 5" from start. Cut yarn and fasten. With front of blouse facing, attach yarn to edge st of collar at center back. Work 1 row of sc around entire neckline, working a sc in top of each dc and 2 sc through ch-2 space on horizontal pattern edge; 3 sc in each dc and ch-3 space along vertical edges; slip st in lower angle of front neckline separation. Work around to starting point, slip st into first sc. Cut yarn and fasten. **Join underside sleeve seams and sides:** Turn blouse to reverse side. Attach yarn at sleeve edges through both layers of fabric. Sc through corner space, sc through top of each dc and 2 sc through ch-2 space, making sure to insert hook through both layers of fabric. *Ch 5, 2 sc through next ch-2 space.* Repeat between *'s across to angle of sleeve. Ch 3, sc through next dc, then join sides together by repeating *sc through ch-3 or dc edge space, ch 3* along side to lower edge. Work opposite side the same. Turn blouse to right side and work 1 row of sc around lower edge of each sleeve. Block to desired measurements.

BABY JACKET in Lattice Shell Pattern

Size: 3–6 months.

Yarn: Knitting worsted; 5 oz.

Hook: Steel ✕00 (or any size required to obtain the stitch gauge given below).

Stitch Gauge: 2 patterns equal 3″; 4 pattern rows equal 2¼″.

Back: Beginning at upper edge, ch 38 and work in Lattice Shell pattern until a total of 6 shell rows has been completed. **Sleeve inset:** Ch 8 (in place of 3), turn and work a shell in 6th ch from hook, dc in top of dc of 6th shell row and continue in pattern across row, omitting last dc at end of row. Instead, ch 3, sc in top of ch 3, ch 6, cut yarn and fasten. Do not turn work; attach yarn to top of ch 3 at left of last shell made, skip 2 chs, shell in next ch, skip 2 chs, dc in last ch. Ch 3, turn work and continue in pattern over these 8 shells until 12 shell rows have been completed below insets. Cut yarn and fasten.

Right Front: Attach yarn at upper right corner of back. Ch 3, shell through base of first shell (of back), dc at base of next dc, shell through base of next shell, dc at base of next dc, ch 3, turn and work in pattern over these 2 shells until a total of 3 rows has been completed. **Shape neckline:** Ch 8, turn and work a shell in 6th ch from hook, dc in next dc and continue pattern over these 3 shells until a total of 3 rows has been completed. **Sleeve inset:** Ch 8, turn and work a shell in 6th ch from hook, dc in next dc and continue pattern over these 4 shells until 12 shell rows have been completed below sleeve inset. Cut yarn and fasten.

Left Front: Attach yarn to corner of upper edge of back on opposite side and work the same as for right front.

Sleeves: Attach yarn to outer tip of 6th shell from starting ch (in angle of sleeve inset). Ch 3, sc in base of shell at right, *work a shell in tip of next shell at left, dc in tip of next shell.* Repeat between *'s across vertical edge of sleeve inset, ending at angle of corresponding sleeve inset (6 shells), working middle dc on shoulder seam instead of shell tip. Sc in base of shell at left, ch 3, turn work, sc in ch 3 at right, then work in pattern over these 6 shells. Sc in ch 3 at left, ch 3, turn work. Continue working in pattern over these 6 shells until a total of 4 rows has been completed. Ch 3, turn work. **Next row:** 3 dc in first shell (a half shell made); work in pattern across next 4 shells, work a half shell in last shell. Ch 3, turn work. **Next row:** Work a half shell in top of first dc of half shell, work in pattern across 4 shells, work a half shell in top of 3rd dc of half shell at end of row. Repeat this last row until 6 rows, beginning and ending with half shells, have been completed. (Sleeve should contain a total of 10 pattern rows from start.) Cut yarn and fasten.

Assembling and Finishing: Sew underarm and side seams on reverse side, catching strands on each edge together using overcast st. Crochet 2 chains, each 12″ long. Tie a single knot in each end of each chain. Insert one through ch-3 spaces at neckline, and the other about 2½″ down center front and tie into bows, as shown in photo. Block or steam press lightly on reverse side.

BOOTEES in Lattice Shell Pattern

Size: 3–6 months.

Yarn: Knitting worsted; 2 oz.

Hook: Steel, ⚹00.

Work as for foot section of Ankle Bootees, Part I, to edging. Ch 3, work Lattice Shell pattern around to starting point. Slip st in top of ch 3; ch 3 and work a 2nd and 3rd round of pattern. Slip st in top of ch 3. Cut yarn and fasten.

Chain Ties: Work the same as for Ankle Bootees, Part II.

CAP in Lattice Shell Pattern

Size: 3–6 months.

Yarn: Knitting worsted; 2 oz.

Hook: Steel, ✕00.

Ch 50 and work in Lattice Shell pattern until 8 rows have been completed. Cut yarn and fasten. Attach yarn to st above dc at left of 3rd shell from right-hand corner of starting ch. Ch 3, skip 2 sts, shell in next st, skip 2 sts, dc in next st, skip 2 sts, shell in next st, skip 2 sts, dc in next 2 sts. Ch 3, turn and work in pattern over these 2 shells until a total of 7 pattern rows has been completed. Cut yarn and fasten. Sew vertical edge of 2-shell strip to horizontal edge of starting ch on each side, using overcast st on what is to be the reverse side. Holding cap upside down, attach yarn to tip of shell at right corner. Ch 4, *dc through next space, ch 1, dc in tip of next shell, ch 1.* Repeat between *'s to 2-shell back section, ending dc through space, ch 1, dc at seam edge, (ch 1, dc through next space, ch 1, dc in ch 2 of shell, ch 1, dc through next space) 2 times, ch 1, dc at seam edge, ch 1, then repeat between *'s across opposite side and end: Ch 1, dc in tip of end shell. Ch 1, turn and work a sc through each ch 1 of previous row. Cut yarn and fasten.

Tie: Make a chain about 28″ long. Run through dc at lower edge of cap, as shown. Tie a single knot in each end of chain.

APRON

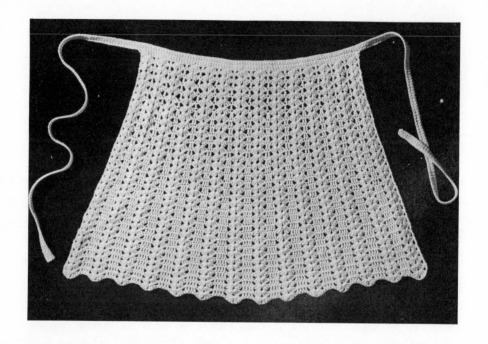

Thread: 2 500-yard balls bedspread cotton, used double strand throughout.

Hook: Steel, 𝕏0.

Using 2 strands together, ch 86 and work in Lattice Shell pattern until 6 shell rows have been completed. Ch 3, turn work. (First section completed.)

Second Section: Row 1: *Shell in next shell, 2 dc in top of next dc.* Repeat between *'s across row, ending last repeat: Shell in last shell, dc in top of ch 3; ch 3, turn work. **Rows 2 through 6:** *Shell in next shell, dc in each of next 2 dc.* Repeat between *'s across row, ending last repeat: Shell in last shell, dc in top of ch 3. Ch 3, turn work.

Third Section: Row 7: *Shell in next shell, dc in top of next dc, dc in space between the 2 dc of previous row, dc in top of next dc.* Repeat between *'s, ending last repeat: Shell in last shell, dc in top of ch 3, ch 3, turn work. **Rows 8 through 12:** *Shell in next shell, dc in top of each of next 3 dc.* Repeat between *'s, ending last repeat: Shell in last shell, dc in top of ch 3. Ch 3, turn work.

Fourth Section: Row 13: *Shell in next shell, dc in top of next dc, 2 dc in top of next dc, dc in top of next dc.* Repeat between *'s across row, ending last repeat: Shell in last shell, dc in top of ch 3. Ch 3, turn work. **Rows 14 through 26:** *Shell in next shell, dc in top of each of next 4 dc.* Repeat between *'s across row, ending last repeat: Shell in last shell, dc in top of ch 3. (32 shell rows now completed from start of work.) **Waistband and ties:** Ch 120, sc in each st across top of apron, ch 121; sc in 2nd ch from hook and in each ch to apron edge. Sc in each st across apron edge and in each ch across opposite side. *Ch 1, turn work, sc in each sc across entire row.* Repeat between *'s until ties measure ½″ wide. Cut thread and fasten. Block or steam press on reverse side.

PUFF SHELL STRIPE

Suggested Uses: Afghans, carriage covers, ski sweaters, hot mats, scatter rugs, ornamental panels, pockets, collars, cuffs.

Starting Chain: Multiple of 6 plus 2. Sc in 2nd ch from hook and in each ch across row. Ch 1, turn work.

Row 1: Sc in first sc, *skip 2 sc; in next sc work 2 dc, 3 tr and 2 dc (a shell made); skip 2 sc, sc in next sc.* Repeat between *'s across row. Ch 3, turn work.

Row 2: (Right side of work) 2 dc in first sc (at base of ch 3), *sc in back loop of middle tr of next shell, 5 dc in next sc.* Repeat between *'s across row and end: 3 dc in last sc. Ch 1, turn work.

Row 3: *Work a shell (as in Row 1) in next sc, skip 2 dc, sc in top of next dc, skip 2 dc.* Repeat between *'s across row, ending: Shell in next sc, skip last 2 dc, sc in top of ch 3. Ch 3, turn work.

Repeat Rows 2 and 3 for pattern.

SHELL AND FILET

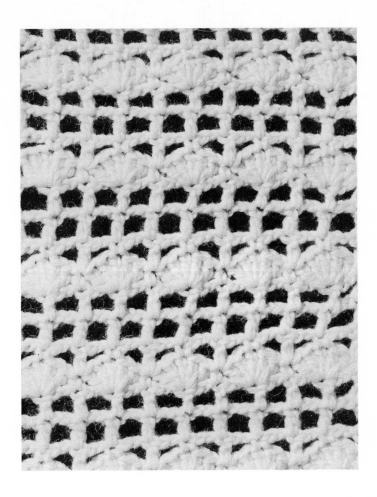

Suggested Uses: Stoles, mufflers, dresses, blouses, place setting mats, table-cloths, bedspreads. This pattern is very attractive when two colors are used; one color for the shell rows and a contrasting color for the filet rows, then turned so that the shells form a series of scalloped stripes running in a vertical direction.

Starting Chain: Multiple of 5 plus 1. Sc in 2nd ch from hook and in each ch across row. Ch 1, turn work.

Starting Row: *Skip 2 sc, 5 dc in next sc (a shell), skip 2 sc, sc in next sc.* Repeat between *'s across row. Ch 5, turn work.

Row 1: *Sc in 3rd dc (middle st) of shell, ch 2, dc in next sc, ch 2.* Repeat between *'s across row, ending last repeat: Dc in ch 1. Ch 5, turn work.

Row 2: *Dc in next sc, ch 2, dc in next dc, ch 2.* Repeat between *'s across row, ending last repeat: Dc in 3rd ch of ch 5. Ch 5, turn work.

Row 3: *Dc in next dc, ch 2.* Repeat between *'s across row, ending: Dc in 3rd ch of ch 5. Ch 1, turn work.

Row 4: *5 dc in next dc, sc in next dc.* Repeat between *'s across row, ending: Sc in 3rd ch of ch 5. Ch 5, turn work.

Repeat from Row 1 for pattern.

EXPANDING SHELL

Suggested Uses: Shrugs, capelets, A-line dresses and blouses, skirts.

Starting Chain: Multiple of 12 plus 3. Sc in 2nd ch from hook and in each ch across row. Ch 3, turn work.

First Row: Skip 3 sc, 3 dc in next sc, ch 2, 3 dc in same sc (a shell made). *Skip 5 sc, work a shell in next sc.* Repeat between *'s across row and end: Skip 3 sc, dc in last sc. Ch 3, turn work.

Expanding Pattern Row 1: *Work a shell through ch 2 of next shell, ch 1, work a shell through ch 2 of next shell.* Repeat between *'s across row and end: Dc in top of ch 3. Repeat this row as many times as necessary before beginning next numbered row.

Expanding Pattern Row 2: Same as Row 1, except: Ch 2 (instead of ch 1). Repeat as many times as necessary.

Expanding Pattern Row 3: Same as Row 1, except: Ch 3 (instead of ch 1).

Expanding Pattern Rows 4 and 5: Same as Row 1, except: Ch 4 on Row 4 and ch 5 on Row 5.

Repeat each pattern row in groups of 2, 3, 4, etc. rows, depending on how wide the last section should be in relation to the width of the first section. For example, the more gradual a slant outward required, the more each row is repeated before going on to the next numbered row. If a very wide slant outward is needed, fewer rows should be repeated. A long garment would require the slant outward to be more gradual than a very short garment. When an expanse of fabric has reached the maximum desired width, the last-numbered row can be repeated as many times as needed to complete a given length, without adding to the width. If additional width is needed, more pattern rows may be added (ch 6, ch 7, etc.) to desired width.

CLUSTER AND SHELL

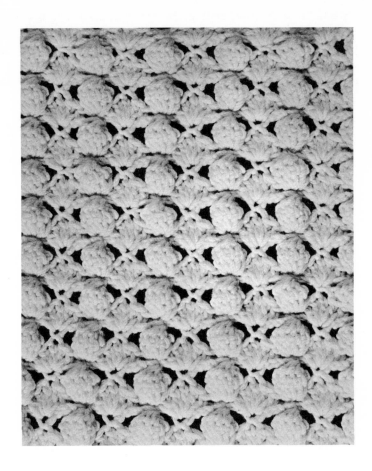

Suggested Uses: Pullovers, cardigans, afghans, carriage covers, bedspreads, stoles, decorative inserts and panels; ornamental collars, cuffs, pockets. An attractive two-color stole or afghan can be made by working Rows 1 and 2 in alternate colors.

Starting Chain: Multiple of 6 plus 3. Sc in 2nd ch from hook and in each ch across row. Ch 3, turn work.

First Row: 2 dc in first sc, *skip 2 sc, sc in next sc, skip 2 sc, 5 dc in next sc (shell made).* Repeat between *'s across row, ending last repeat: 3 dc in last sc (instead of 5). Ch 1, turn work.

Row 1 (reverse side): Sc in first dc, *ch 3; holding back last loop of each tr on hook, work 5 tr in next sc, then draw yarn through all 6 loops on hook (a cluster made); ch 3, sc in 3rd (middle) dc of next shell.* Repeat between *'s across row, ending: Sc in top of ch 3. Ch 3, turn work.

Row 2: 2 dc in first sc, *sc in tip of next cluster, 5 dc in next sc.* Repeat between *'s across row, ending last repeat: 3 dc in sc (instead of 5). Ch 1, turn work.

Repeat Rows 1 and 2 for pattern.

SHELLY LACE

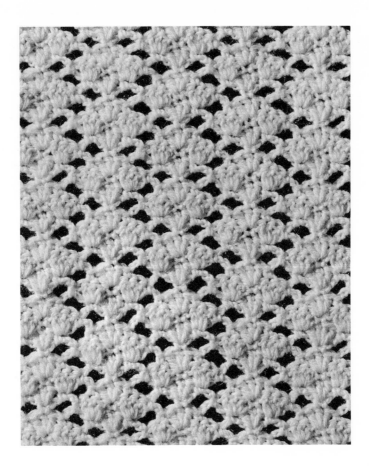

Suggested Uses: Dresses, blouses, stoles, mufflers, place setting mats, tablecloths, carriage covers, ornamental collars and panels.

Starting Chain: Multiple of 8 plus 2. Sc in 2nd ch from hook and in each ch across row. Ch 1, turn work.
Starting Row A: Sc in first st, *ch 4, skip 3 sc, sc in next st.* Repeat between *'s across row. Ch 3, turn work.
Starting Row B: Dc in first sc (half shell) *sc through next ch 4, (ch 4, sc in next ch 4) 3 times; 3 dc in next sc (shell).* Repeat between *'s across row, ending: 2 dc in last sc. Ch 1, turn work.

Starting Row C: Sc in first dc, shell in next sc, *sc through next ch 4, (ch 4, sc through next ch 4) 2 times, shell in next sc, sc in middle dc of next shell, shell in next sc.* Repeat between *'s across row and end: Sc in top of ch 3. Ch 3, turn work.

Row 1: Dc in first sc, *sc in middle dc of next shell, ch 4, sc through next ch 4, shell in next sc, sc through next ch 4, ch 4, sc in middle dc of next shell, shell in next sc.* Repeat between *'s across row, ending: 2 dc in last sc. Ch 1, turn work.

Row 2: Sc in first dc, *ch 4, sc through next ch 4, shell in next sc, sc in middle dc of next shell, shell in next sc, sc through next ch 4, ch 4, sc in middle dc of next shell.* Repeat between *'s across row, ending last repeat: Sc in top of ch 3. Ch 3, turn work.

Row 3: Dc in first sc, *sc through next ch 4, ch 4, sc in middle dc of next shell, shell in next sc, sc in middle dc of next shell, ch 4, sc through next ch 4, shell in next sc.* Repeat between *'s across row, ending: 2 dc in last sc. Ch 1, turn work.

Row 4: Sc in first dc, *shell in next sc, sc through next ch 4, ch 4, sc in middle dc of next shell, ch 4, sc through next ch 4, shell in next sc, sc in middle dc of next shell.* Repeat between *'s across row, ending: Sc in top of ch 3. Ch 3, turn work.

Repeat Rows 1 through 4 for desired length and end as follows:

Finishing Row A: Dc in first sc, *sc in middle dc of next shell, (ch 4, sc through next ch 4) 2 times, ch 4, sc in middle dc of next shell, shell in next sc.* Repeat between *'s across row, ending: 2 dc in last sc. Ch 1, turn work.

Finishing Row B: Sc in first dc, *(ch 4, sc in next ch 4) 3 times, ch 4, sc in middle dc of next shell.* Repeat between *'s across row, ending: Sc in top of ch 3. Cut yarn and fasten.

DIAGONAL SHELL

Suggested Uses: Carriage covers, blouses, dresses, women's vests, stoles, decorative inserts, panels and edgings. This pattern creates an interesting striped effect when two different colors are alternated between Rows 1 and 2, then turned so that the shells run in vertical formation. A simple cap-sleeve shift in two colors can be made by working the starting chain and single crochet rows a few inches longer than the desired dress length, then working the first pattern row to desired length. Change colors between Rows 1 and 2, working to proper dress width, which should be about 2″ wider each side than half the hip or bust measurement, whichever is larger. Sew narrow edges together on one end for shoulder seams, leaving a 9″ opening in middle for neckline. Sew side seams, block to desired measurements, and you have just about as attractive a spring and summer shift as one could imagine. Use a medium or lightweight yarn and any size crochet hook that will comfortably accommodate the yarn; 18 to 20 oz of yarn should be enough.

Starting Chain: Multiple of 4 plus 1. Sc in 2nd ch from hook and in each ch across row. Ch 4, turn work.

Next Row: Skip 3 sc, sc in next sc, *ch 4, skip 3 sc, sc in next sc.* Repeat between *'s across row. Ch 4, turn work.

Row 1: *2 tr through next ch 4, ch 1; (yarn over hook, insert hook through space at right of 2nd tr from hook, complete a dc) 4 times.* Repeat between *'s across row, working a motif in last ch-4 loop at edge. Ch 4, turn work.

Row 2 (right side): Skip 3 dc, sc in top of next dc, *ch 4, skip 3 dc in next motif, sc in top of 4th dc.* Repeat between *'s across row. Ch 4, turn work.

Repeat Rows 1 and 2 for pattern.

EMBOSSED SHELL

Suggested Uses: Ski sweaters, carriage covers, afghans, tote bags.

A particularly attractive pattern when each row is done in a different color.

Starting Chain: Multiple of 6 plus 1. Sc in 2nd ch from hook and in each ch across row. Ch 1, turn work.

First Row: *Skip next 2 sc; in next sc work 3 tr, ch 2, 3 tr; skip next 2 sc, sc in next sc.* Repeat between *'s across row. Ch 4, turn work.

Row 1 (right side): 2 tr in back loop of first sc (at base of ch 4), sc through next ch 2, *5 tr in back loop of next sc, sc through next ch 2.* Repeat between *'s across row and end: 3 tr in ch 1 of previous row. Ch 1, turn work.

Row 2: *In next sc, work 3 tr, ch 2, 3 tr; skip next 2 tr, sc in next tr.* Repeat between *'s across row, ending: Sc in top of ch 4 of previous row. Ch 4, turn work.

Repeat Rows 1 and 2 for pattern.

FAN SHELL

Suggested Uses: Baby wear, carriage covers, pullovers, cardigans, afghans, tote bags.

Starting Chain: Multiple of 6 plus 1. Sc in 2nd ch from hook and in each ch across row. Ch 1, turn work.

First Row: *Skip 2 sc, 7 dc in next sc (a shell made), skip 2 sc, sc in next sc.* Repeat between *'s across row. Ch 3, turn work.

Row 1: 3 dc at base of ch 3, *sc in back loop of 4th (middle) dc of next shell, 7 dc in back loop of next sc.* Repeat between *'s across row, ending: 4 dc in ch 1 of previous row. Ch 1, turn work.

Row 2 (reverse side): *7 dc in front loop of next sc, sc in front loop of 4th (middle) dc of next shell.* Repeat between *'s across row, ending: 7 dc in front loop of next sc, sc in top of ch 3. Ch 3, turn work.

Repeat Rows 1 and 2 for pattern.

TWO-COLOR REVERSE SHELL

Suggested Uses: Afghans, place setting mats, hot mats, tote bags, decorator pillows, pullovers, jackets, ornamental collars, cuffs, pockets.

Starting Chain: Multiple of 11 plus 1, using light color. Sc in 2nd ch from hook and in each ch across row. Ch 3, turn work.

Next Row: 3 dc in first sc (half shell made), *skip 3 sc, 7 dc in next sc (a shell made), skip 3 sc, sc in next sc.* Repeat between *'s across row and end: Skip 3 sc, 4 dc in last sc (half shell made). Cut light color, attach dark color, ch 1, turn work.

81

Row 1 (right side of work): Sc and ch 3 in first dc; *holding back last loop on hook of each dc, work dc in same st as ch 3, in next 3 dc, in next sc and in next 4 dc, draw yarn through all 10 loops on hook and ch 1 snugly; ch 3, sc in same st as last dc was worked (a reverse shell made), ch 3.* Repeat between *'s across row, ending last dc in top of ch 3; ch 3, sc in same st. Ch 1, turn work.

Row 2: *Work a shell (7 dc) in middle of next reverse shell, sc in next sc.* Repeat between *'s across row, ending last sc in base of ch 3. Cut dark color, attach light color, ch 3, turn work.

Row 3: Holding back last loop of each dc, work dc in base of ch 3 and in next 4 dc, draw yarn through all 6 loops on hook, ch 1 snugly, ch 3, dc in same st as last dc was worked (half reverse shell made); *ch 3, work a reverse shell (as in Row 1).* Repeat between *'s across row, ending: Ch 3; holding back last loop of each dc, work dc in base of ch 3 and in next 3 dc, draw yarn through all 5 loops on hook, ch 1 (half reverse shell made). Ch 3, turn work.

Row 4: Work a half shell (3 dc) in base of ch 3, *sc in next sc, work a shell (7 dc) in middle of next reverse shell.* Repeat between *'s across row and end: Sc in next sc, 4 dc in top of half reverse shell. Cut light color, attach dark color, ch 1, turn work.

Repeat from Row 1 for pattern.

EMBOSSED APPLE BLOSSOM

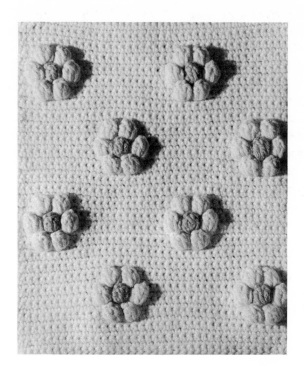

Suggested Uses: Decorative pillows, scatter rugs, tote bags, ornamental collars, cuffs, pockets, edgings, inserts, panels. Use this unusual pattern in lightweight wool for footstool and fireside bench upholstery fabric. Pattern in photo was made with white, pink and green; however, any desired color combination can be used.

Starting Chain: Multiple of 20 plus 2. Sc in 2nd ch from hook and in each ch across row, using white or desired ground color. Ch 1, turn work. Work Popcorn Stitch, when so directed below, as follows: 5 dc in next st, drop loop from hook and insert in top of first dc made, pull loop through, ch 1.
Rows 1 through 6: Sc in each st across row. Ch 1, turn work.

Row 7: Sc in each of next 4 sts, *cut white, attach pink with a firm double knot at back of hook; popcorn st in next st, sc in next st, popcorn st in next st; cut pink, attach white, sc in each of next 17 sts.* Repeat between *'s across row, ending last repeat: 14 sc (instead of 17). Ch 1, turn work.

Row 8: Sc in each sc and in top of each popcorn st across row, taking care that row contains a multiple of 20 plus 1. Ch 1, turn work.

Row 9: Sc in each of next 3 sts, *cut white, attach pink; popcorn st in next st, sc in next st, cut pink, attach green, popcorn st in next st; cut green, attach pink, sc in next st, popcorn st in next st, cut pink, attach white, sc in each of next 15 sts.* Repeat between *'s across row, ending last repeat: 13 sc (instead of 15). Ch 1, turn work.

Row 10: Same as Row 8.

Row 11: Same as Row 7.

Rows 12 through 18: Same as Row 8.

Row 19: Sc in each of 14 sts, then work between *'s as in Row 7, ending last repeat: Sc in each of last 4 sts.

Row 20: Same as Row 8.

Row 21: Sc in each of 13 sts, then work between *'s as in Row 9, ending last repeat: Sc in last 3 sts. Ch 1, turn work.

Row 22: Same as Row 8.

Row 23: Same as Row 19.

Row 24: Same as Row 8.

Repeat from Row 1 for desired length.

DECORATOR PILLOW in Embossed
Apple Blossom Pattern
(Not illustrated)

Size: 12″ square, exclusive of fringe.

Yarn: Knitting worsted; 8 oz white, 2 oz pink, 1 oz green.

Hook: Size F (or any size required to obtain the stitch gauge given below).

Stitch Gauge: 9 sc sts equal 2″.

Pillow Form: 12″ square.

Make 2: Using white, ch 62 and work in Embossed Apple Blossom pattern until piece measures approximately 13″, ending on Row 6 or 18 (piece should be as long as it is wide). Block each piece. Using white, and with right sides turned out, join edges on 3 sides with a row of sc, working 3 sc in each corner and making sure that hook penetrates both layers of fabric. Insert pillow form, then join edges along 4th side with a row of sc. Attach 2″ fringe around all sides, if desired.

PINE TREE PATTERN

Suggested Uses: Ski sweaters, scatter rugs, hats, tote bags, decorator pillows, ornamental collars, cuffs, pockets, edgings, borders, panels, upholstery fabric for fireside benches, hassocks, etc.

Starting Chain: Multiple of 16 plus 2. Sc in 2nd ch from hook and in each ch across row. Ch 1, turn work. Work popcorn st in directions below as follows: 4 dc in next st; remove hook from loop and insert in top of first dc made, then insert hook in loop at back and pull through, ch 1.

Rows 1 through 6: Sc in each st across row. Ch 1, turn work.

Row 7: Sc in next 2 sts, *cut main color, attach green with a firm double knot resting snug against back of hook; popcorn st in next st, sc in next st, popcorn st in next st, sc in next st, popcorn st in next st, cut green, attach main color, sc in next 11 sts.* Repeat between *'s across row, ending last repeat: Sc in last 10 sts. Ch 1, turn work.

Row 8: Sc in each sc across row (and in top of each popcorn st), taking care that row contains a multiple of 16 sts plus 1. Ch 1, turn work.

Row 9: Sc in next 3 sts, *cut main color, attach green, popcorn st in next st, sc in next st, popcorn st in next st, cut green, attach main color, sc in next 13 sts.* Repeat between *'s across row, ending last repeat: Sc in last 11 sts. Ch 1, turn work.

Row 10: Same as Row 8.

Row 11: Sc in next 4 sts, *cut main color, attach green, popcorn st in next st, cut green, attach main color, sc in next 15 sts.* Repeat between *'s across row, ending last repeat: Sc in last 12 sts. Ch 1, turn work.

Rows 12 through 24: Same as Row 8.

Row 25: Sc in next 10 sts, then repeat directions between *'s in Row 7 across row, ending last repeat: Sc in last 2 sts.

Row 26: Same as Row 8.

Row 27: Sc in next 11 sts, then repeat directions between *'s in Row 9 across row, ending last repeat: Sc in last 3 sts. Ch 1, turn work.

Row 28: Same as Row 8.

Row 29: Sc in next 12 sts, then repeat directions between *'s in Row 11 across row, ending last repeat: Sc in last 4 sts.

Rows 30 through 36: Same as Row 8.

Repeat from Row 1 for desired length. Using green yarn, embroider a chain st for "tree trunk" at base of each group of popcorn sts, as shown.

YARN FLOWER PICTURE

Size: About 11½"×16", unframed.

Yarn: Knitting worsted; 3 oz ground color, 1 oz brown, ½ oz each of 2 flower colors, 4 yards green.

Hook: Aluminum size G.

Row 1: Using ground color, ch 46, sc in 2nd ch from hook and in each ch across row. Ch 1, turn work.

Rows 2 through 11: Sc in each sc across row. Ch 1, turn work.

Row 12: Sc in each of 19 sts; cut ground color, attach brown with a firm square knot which rests snug against back of hook; work 5 dc in next sc, remove hook from loop, insert hook through first dc made, then pull loop through (a popcorn st made), *ch 1, work a popcorn st in next sc, sc in next sc.* Work between *'s 3 times, to total 4 popcorn sts in this row; cut brown, attach ground color, ch 1, sc in each sc across row. Ch 1, turn work.

Rows 13 and all odd-numbered rows: Sc in each sc across row in ground color only, working 1 sc in back of each popcorn st, and making sure that each row contains 45 sts. Ch 1, turn work.

Rows 14, 16, 18 and 20: Sc in each across to (but not including) sc directly to the right of first popcorn st; cut ground color, attach brown and work between *'s in Row 12 until there is a total of one more popcorn st in row than in previous right-side row. Cut brown, attach ground color. (This is the "flower pot" and the 20th row should contain 8 popcorn sts with a ch 1 and sc between. See photo.)

Rows 22 through 29: Work all rows as for reverse side.

Row 30: Sc in each of 11 sts, cut ground color, attach first flower color; work a popcorn st in next st, ch 1, sc in next st, work a popcorn st in next st, cut first flower color, attach ground color, ch 1, sc in each st across row.

Row 32: Sc in each of 10 sts, cut ground color, attach first flower color, work a popcorn st in next st, ch 1, sc in next st, cut first flower color, attach green, work a popcorn st in next st, ch 1, sc in next st, cut green, attach first flower color, work a popcorn st in next st, cut first flower color, attach ground color, ch 1, sc in each st across row. Ch 1, turn work.

Row 34: Same as Row 30. (Refer to photo.)

Row 36: Sc across 31 sts, cut ground color, attach second flower color, work a popcorn st in next st, ch 1, sc in next st, work a popcorn st in next st, cut second flower color, attach ground color, ch 1, sc in each st across row. Ch 1, turn work.

Row 38: Sc across 30 sts, cut ground color, attach second flower color, work a popcorn st in next st, ch 1, sc in next st, cut second flower color, attach green, work a popcorn st in next st, ch 1, sc in next st, cut green, attach second flower color, work a popcorn st in next st, cut second flower color, attach ground color, ch 1, sc in each st across row. Ch 1, turn work.

Row 40: Same as Row 36.

Rows 42, 44 and 46: Using second flower color, repeat Rows 30, 32 and 34 (another flower made on right-hand side of fabric).

Rows 48, 50 and 52: Using first flower color, repeat Rows 36, 38 and 40 (another flower made on left-hand side of fabric).

Continue as above until one more flower is made on each side of picture, using first flower color on right-hand side and second flower color on left-hand side, then work in sc st across each row with a ch 1 to turn, for 11 more rows. Cut yarn and fasten.

Using brown, work stems in embroidered chain st. Using green, work a large chain st at the 2 positions shown for leaves, then work a larger chain st in brown around the green chain st.

Block picture to precise rectangular shape, cement with white fabric glue to a piece of very heavy cardboard of exact size as picture. Place in frame, if desired.

EMBOSSED DIAMOND STRIPE

Suggested Uses: Winter coats and cardigans, afghan panels, handbags, tote bags, decorative pillows, ornamental collars, cuffs, panels, pockets.

Starting Chain: Multiple of 10 plus 2. Sc in 2nd ch from hook and in each ch across row. Ch 1, turn work.

Row 1: Sc in each of next 5 sts, *5 dc in next st, remove hook from loop and insert in first dc made, then insert hook in loop at back and pull loop through, ch 1 (a popcorn st made), sc in each of next 9 sts.* Repeat between *'s across row, ending last repeat: Sc in each of last 5 sts. Ch 1, turn work.

Row 2: Sc in each of next 5 sts, *ch 1, skip next st, sc in each of next 9 sts.* Repeat between *'s across row, ending last repeat: Sc in each of last 5 sts. Ch 1, turn work.

Row 3: Sc in each of next 4 sts, *work a popcorn st in next st, sc in ch 1 of previous row, popcorn st in next st, sc in each of next 7 sts.* Repeat between *'s across row, ending last repeat: Sc in each of last 4 sts. Ch 1, turn work.

Row 4: Sc in each of next 4 sts, *ch 1, skip next st, sc in next st, ch 1, skip next st, sc in each of next 7 sts.* Repeat between *'s across row, ending last repeat: Sc in each of last 4 sts. Ch 1, turn work.

Row 5: Sc in each of next 3 sts, *work a popcorn st in next st, sc in ch 1 of previous row, work a popcorn st in next st, sc in ch 1 of previous row, work a popcorn st in next st, sc in each of next 5 sts.* Repeat between *'s across row, ending last repeat: Sc in each of last 3 sts. Ch 1, turn work.

Row 6: Sc in each of next 3 sts, *ch 1, skip next st, sc in next st, ch 1, skip next st, sc in next st, ch 1, sc in each of next 5 sts.* Repeat between *'s across row, ending last repeat: Sc in each of last 3 sts. Ch 1, turn work.

Row 7: Same as Row 3.

Row 8: Same as Row 4.

Repeat from Row 1 for pattern, ending on a Row 2 for uniformity.

POPCORN FILET

Suggested Uses: Cardigans, pullovers, blouses, afghans, bedspreads, coverlets, carriage covers, mufflers, stoles, shawls, ponchos.

Starting Chain: Multiple of 10 plus 9. Dc in 4th ch from hook, *ch 2, skip 2 ch, dc in next ch.* Repeat between *'s across row and end: Work another dc in last ch. Ch 3, turn work.

Row 1: 5 dc in top of 2nd dc; remove hook from loop and insert through top of first dc made in this group of 5, then insert hook in loop and pull loop through at back, ch 1 (a popcorn st made), *ch 2, dc in top of next dc, ch 2, work a popcorn st in top of next dc.* Repeat between *'s across row, ending last repeat: Ch 2, dc in last dc, dc in top of ch 3. Ch 3, turn work.

Row 2: Dc in top of 2nd dc, *ch 2, dc in top of next popcorn st, ch 2, dc in top of next dc.* Repeat between *'s across row and end: Ch 2, dc in top of last popcorn st, dc in top of ch 3. Ch 3, turn work.

Row 3: Dc in top of 2nd dc, *ch 2, popcorn st in top of next dc, ch 2, dc in top of next dc.* Repeat between *'s across row, ending last repeat: Ch 2, popcorn st in last dc, dc in top of ch 3. Ch 3, turn work.

Row 4: *Dc in top of popcorn st, ch 2, dc in top of next dc, ch 2.* Repeat between *'s across row, ending last repeat: Omit last ch 2, dc in top of ch 3. Ch 3, turn work.

Repeat from Row 1 for pattern.

LACY DIADEM

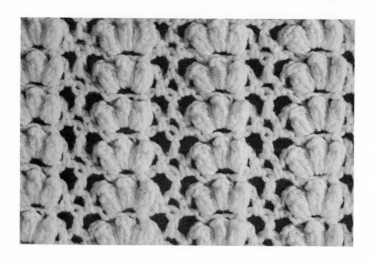

Suggested Uses: Afghans, carriage covers, stoles, blouses, cardigans, decorative panels and collars.

Starting Chain: Multiple of 9 plus 1. Sc in 2nd ch from hook in each ch across row. Ch 3, turn work. In directions below, work a popcorn st, where called for, as follows: Work 4 dc in space as directed; remove hook from loop, insert through first dc made and pull loop through.

First Row: *Skip 2 sc, sc in next sc, ch 4, skip 2 sc, sc in next sc, ch 3, skip 2 sc, sc in next sc, ch 3.* Repeat between *'s across row, ending: Ch 3, sc in last sc. Ch 3, turn work.

Row 1: *Sc through next ch loop, ch 3, popcorn st through next ch loop, ch 2, popcorn st in same ch loop, ch 2, popcorn st in same ch loop, ch 3, sc in next ch loop, ch 3.* Repeat between *'s across row, ending: Sc in last ch loop. Ch 5, turn work.

Row 2: Sc through next ch loop, ch 2, skip next ch loop, sc through next ch loop, *ch 4, sc through next ch loop, ch 2, skip next ch loop, dc through next ch loop, ch 2, skip next ch loop, sc through next ch loop.* Repeat between *'s across row, ending: Ch 4, sc through next ch loop, ch 2, skip next ch loop, dc through last ch loop. Ch 3, turn work.

Repeat Rows 1 and 2 for pattern.

TWO-COLOR POPCORN STRIPE

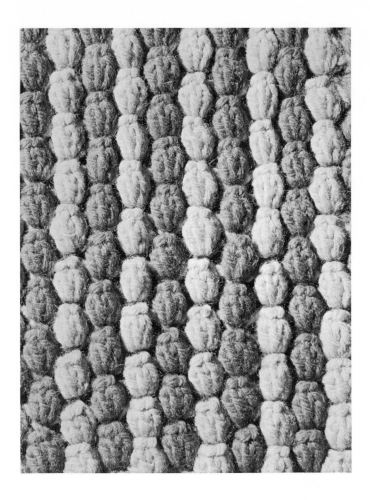

Suggested Uses: Handbags, tote bags, decorative pillows, scatter rugs, hot mats, alternate afghan panels, ornamental collars, cuffs, pockets, heavy ski sweaters, winter jackets.

Starting Chain: Multiple of 8 plus 2. Using light color, sc in 2nd ch from hook and in each ch across row. Ch 1, turn work.

First Row: Continuing in light color, sc in each of first 2 sts, *ch 2, skip next st, 5 dc in next st; remove hook from loop and insert in first dc made, then insert hook in loop at back and pull loop through, ch 1 (a popcorn st made), ch 2, skip next st, sc in next st.* Repeat between *'s across row, ending last repeat: Ch 2, skip next st, work a popcorn st in next st, dc in last st. Cut yarn and fasten. Do not turn work.

Row 1: With right side facing, attach dark color to first sc made. Ch 3, work a popcorn st in next st, *ch 2, sc in back st at top of next popcorn st, ch 2, work a popcorn st in next sc.* Repeat between *'s across row and end: Ch 2, sc in last popcorn st, sc in top of dc. Cut yarn and fasten. Do not turn work.

Row 2: With right side facing, attach light color to top of ch 3 made at beginning of row. Sc in same space, sc in top of first popcorn st, *ch 2, work a popcorn st in next sc, ch 2, sc in back st at top of next popcorn st.* Repeat between *'s across row, ending: Ch 2, work a popcorn st in next sc, dc in last st. Cut yarn and fasten. Do not turn work.

Repeat Rows 1 and 2 for pattern.

TREBLE AND POPCORN

Suggested Uses: Ornamental collars, cuffs, pockets, panels, and as an edge trim for cardigans, pullovers, blouses, dresses, stoles.

Starting Chain: Multiple of 3. Sc in 2nd ch from hook and in each ch across row. Ch 1, turn work. For 2-color fabric, as shown, work each Row 1 in contrasting color.

Row 1: Sc in each of next 2 sts, *5 dc in next st, remove hook from loop and insert through top of first dc made, then insert hook in loop and pull through, ch 1 (a popcorn st made), sc in each of next 2 sts.* Repeat between *'s across row. Ch 1, turn work.

Row 2: Sc in each of next 2 sts, *ch 1, skip popcorn st, sc in each of next 2 sts.* Repeat between *'s across row. Ch 4, turn work.

Row 3: Tr in sc at right of first popcorn st, *ch 1, skip ch 1 over popcorn st, tr in each of next 2 sts.* Repeat between *'s across row. Ch 1, turn work.

Row 4: Sc in each of next 2 sts, *sc through next ch 1, sc in each of next 2 sts.* Repeat between *'s across row, ending last sc in top of ch 4. Ch 1, turn work.

Repeat from Row 1 for pattern.

TREBLE FILET

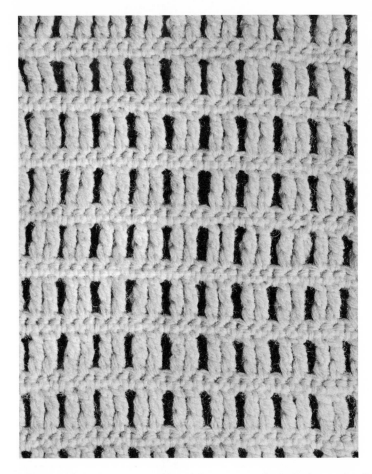

Suggested Uses: Alternate panels for afghans, coverlets, bedspreads, draperies, or combine with Treble and Popcorn pattern for blouses, dresses, stoles, pullovers.

Starting Chain: Multiple of 3. Sc in 2nd ch from hook and in each ch across row. Ch 1, turn work.

Row 1: Sc in first st, ch 4, tr in next st, *ch 1, skip next st, tr in each of next 2 sts.* Repeat between *'s across row. Ch 1, turn work.

Row 2: Sc in each of next 2 sts, *sc through next ch 1, sc in each of next 2 sts.* Repeat between *'s across row, ending last sc in top of ch 4. Repeat Rows 1 and 2 for pattern.

BOBBLE AND STRIPE

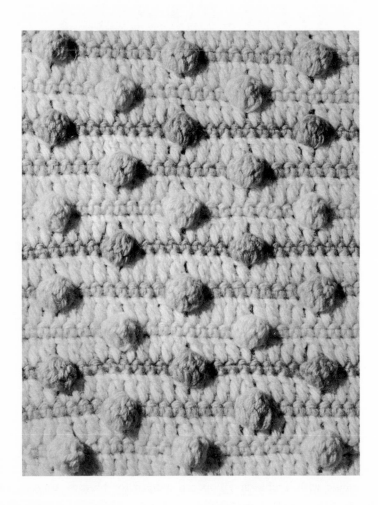

Suggested Uses: Baby wear, carriage covers, afghans, cardigans, tote bags, handbags, hats, ornamental edgings, collars, cuffs, panels.

Starting Chain: Multiple of 10 plus 3. Using white or desired main color, sc in 2nd ch from hook and in each ch across row; ch 1, turn work. Work a bobble in directions below as follows: (Yarn over hook, draw loop through st, draw yarn through first 2 loops on hook) 5 times in same st, then draw yarn through all 6 loops on hook, ch 1.

First Row: Continuing in white, sc in first st, ch 3, dc in each st across row.

Row 1: Cut white, attach a color, ch 1, turn work. Sc in next 3 sts, *work a bobble in next st, sc in next 9 sts.* Repeat between *'s across row, ending last repeat: Sc in each of last 7 sts, sc in top of ch 3. Cut color, attach white, ch 1, turn work.

Row 2: Sc in first st, ch 3, dc in each of next 7 sts, *skip ch 1 of bobble, dc in last loop at left of bobble, dc in each of next 9 sts.* Repeat between *'s across row, ending last repeat: Dc in left bobble loop, dc in each of last 3 sts. Cut white, attach a color, ch 1, turn work.

Row 3: Sc in next 8 sts, then repeat directions between *'s in Row 1, ending last repeat: Work a bobble in next st, sc in each of next 2 sts, sc in top of ch 3. Cut color, attach white, ch 1, turn work.

Row 4: Sc in first st, ch 3, dc in each of next 2 sts, repeat between *'s in Row 2, ending last repeat: Dc in left bobble loop, dc in each of last 8 sts. Repeat from Row 1 for pattern.

QUICK AND EASY CAP-SLEEVE DRESSES
AND BLOUSES in Any Suitable Pattern

Attractive cap-sleeve dresses can be made from any suitable pattern in Parts III and IV in the same way that the two-piece stole is made. It is advisable to use nothing heavier in weight than knitting worsted for winter wear and lightweight dress yarn or fingering yarn for spring and summer dresses.

The amount of yarn required varies according to the pattern selected; however, the average pattern (not too lacy and not too heavy) will require about 24 to 30 oz of knitting worsted and about 18 to 20 oz of dress weight, light sports or fingering yarn. Use any size of hook that will comfortably accommodate the yarn selected.

As in crocheting a stole without a specific set of instructions, a simple cap-sleeve dress may be started by either working a foundation chain of the desired width and then adjusting to the proper pattern multiple, or working the chain several inches longer than is required, then working the first row of pattern across to the desired width and cutting away the extra length of chain about ½″ from the end of the pattern row. If the pattern is in squares or other joined motifs, these can be joined across the first row to the proper width, then proceed with the same number of motifs across each row to the desired dress length.

To determine the width needed for each side of the dress, measure hips and bust, use the larger measurement of the two, divide this number in half, and to this last figure add 2 inches additional width. For example: If the hip measurement is the larger and measures 40″, divide the 40″ in half, making 20″, add 2″. This will total 22″. Each side of the dress should measure 22″ across. If a very loose fitting dress is desired, then another inch may be added to the width of each side.

After the width of each side has been determined, work in pattern until piece measures the desired dress length when measured from shoulder seam to lower edge, bearing in mind that very lacy or loosely crocheted fabrics often drop 2″ or 3″ after being blocked or laundered.

When both pieces have been completed, making sure that each side contains exactly the same number of pattern rows, place right sides together and sew shoulder seams, leaving a 9″ or 9½″ opening in the middle for neckline. Use either the overcast st or running backstitch for sewing, depending on which is more suitable for a specific pattern. Sew side seams, leaving an arm opening each side of desired length. Small

102

sizes should have an arm opening of about 6½″ or 7″, medium, 7″ or 7½″, and large, about 8″ or 8½″. If the pattern used has no definite edging of its own, work 2 or 3 rows of single crochet around neckline and arm openings. The lower edge can either be finished with 2 or 3 rows of single crochet, or it may be hemmed in the same way that one would hem a garment of woven material. Block to desired measurements.

This simple dress may be worn as a skimmer, or with a tie at the waist. For a matching tie, use two or three strands of yarn together and crochet a chain to desired length. Tie a single knot in each end and trim excess just below each knot. Small pompons or tassels may be attached to the ends of the waist tie, if desired.

A cap-sleeve blouse or Toga Top (see next four pages) can be made in exactly the same way by working each side to desired length. About 18 to 20 oz of knitting worsted or 14 oz of lightweight yarn will be required; small sizes may use slightly less and larger sizes may use more, depending upon length and width of garment and pattern selected.

FANFARE PATTERN

Suggested Uses: Dresses, blouses, bedspreads, stoles, mufflers, place setting mats, afghans, decorative panels and inserts.

Starting Chain: Multiple of 10 plus 2. Sc in 2nd ch from hook and in each ch across row. Ch 3, turn work.

Row 1: Skip first st, *dc in each of next 2 sts, ch 3, skip 2 sts, sc in next st, ch 3, skip 2 sts, dc in each of next 3 sts.* Repeat between *'s across row (ending last dc in top of turning ch of previous row on all Row 1 repeats after the first). Ch 3, turn work.

Row 2: Skip first dc, *dc in next 2 sts, ch 1, sc in ch-3 space, ch 3, sc in next ch-3 space, ch 1, dc in next 3 sts.* Repeat between *'s across row, ending last dc in top of turning ch of previous row. Ch 3, turn work.

Row 3: Skip first dc, *dc in each of next 2 dc, 5 dc in ch-3 space, dc in each of next 3 dc.* Repeat between *'s across row, ending last dc in top of turning ch of previous row. Ch 3, turn work.

Repeat from Row 1 for pattern.

TOGA TOP in Fanfare Pattern

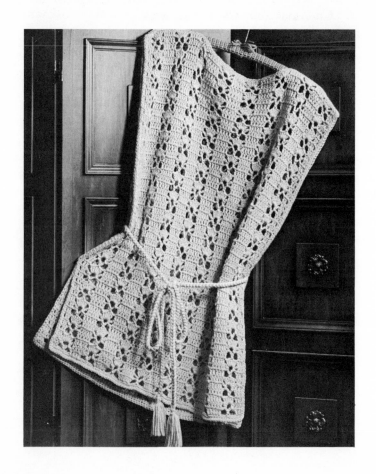

Size: Directions are given first for medium (size 34″–36″ bust). Changes for larger sizes (38″–40″, 42″–44″) follow in parentheses.

Yarn: Knitting worsted; 20 oz.

Hook: Aluminum size F (or any size required to obtain the stitch gauge given below).

Stitch Gauge: 2 patterns (over 20 sts) equal 5¼″.

Back and Front are identical; make 2 of the following: Beginning at upper edge, ch 72 (82, 92) loosely and work in Fanfare pattern until piece measures 25″ from start (or desired length from shoulder seam to lower edge), making sure that both front and back contain the same number of pattern rows.

Steam press each piece lightly on reverse side. Work 1 row sc around entire outside edge of each piece, working 3 sc in each corner. Sew shoulder seams, leaving a 9″ opening in middle for neckline. Sew side seams, leaving a 7″ (7½″, 8″) opening at upper portion for arm openings and a 6″ mandarin slit each side at lower edge.

Waist Tie: Using 3 strands of yarn together, crochet a chain about 44″ long. Tie a single knot in each end. A tassel can be attached to ends of chain, as shown, if desired.

BUTTERFLY AND BLOCK

Suggested Uses: Stoles, mufflers, women's vests, carriage covers, bedspreads, place setting mats, tablecloths. A beautiful tablecloth can be made from this pattern, using bedspread cotton either single strand with a steel size 1 or 2 hook, or double strand using a size 0 or 00 hook. The amount of cotton thread needed depends on the size of the tablecloth, and whether it is done with 1 or 2 strands. About 16 500-yard balls should make an average-size cloth when used double strand.

Starting Chain: Multiple of 20 plus 4. Sc in 2nd ch from hook and in each ch across row. Ch 3, turn work.

First Row: *Dc in each of next 10 sts, ch 10, skip next 10 sts.* Repeat between *'s across row, ending: Dc in each of last 2 sts. Ch 3, turn work.

Row 1: Dc in top of 2nd dc, *ch 10, dc in top of each of next 4 dc, ch 2, skip next 2 dc, dc in top of each of next 4 dc.* Repeat between *'s across row, ending: Dc in top of ch 3. Ch 3, turn work.

Row 2: *Dc in top of each of next 2 dc, ch 2, skip next 2 dc, 2 dc through next ch-2 space, ch 2, skip next 2 dc, dc in top of each of next 2 dc, ch 10.* Repeat between *'s across row, ending: Dc in next dc, dc in top of ch 3. Ch 3, turn work.

Row 3: Dc in top of 2nd dc, *ch 5, sc through all 3 ch (together) of previous 3 rows, ch 5, dc in top of each of next 2 dc, 2 dc through next ch-2 space, ch 2, 2 dc through next ch-2 space, dc in top of each of next 2 dc.* Repeat between *'s across row, ending: Dc in top of ch 3. Ch 3, turn work.

Row 4: *Dc in top of each of next 4 dc, 2 dc in next ch-2 space, dc in top of each of next 4 dc, ch 10.* Repeat between *'s across row, ending: Dc in top of last dc, dc in top of ch 3. Ch 3, turn work.

Row 5: Dc in top of 2nd dc, *dc in next 10 ch, ch 10.* Repeat between *'s across row, ending: Dc in top of last dc, dc in top of ch 3. Ch 3, turn work. Repeat from Row 1 for pattern.

GRECIAN LACE

Suggested Uses: Tablecloths, bedspreads, place setting mats, draperies, stoles, carriage covers.

Starting Chain: Multiple of 11 plus 3. Dc in 4th ch from hook, *ch 8, skip next 8 ch, dc in each of next 3 ch.* Repeat between *'s across row, ending last repeat: Dc in each of last 2 ch. Ch 3, turn work.

Row 1: Dc in top of 2nd dc, *ch 8, dc in top of each of next 3 dc.* Repeat between *'s across row, ending: Dc in top of last dc, dc in top of ch 3. Ch 3, turn work.

Row 2: Same as Row 1.

Row 3: Dc in top of 2nd dc, *ch 4, sc through all 3 ch (together) of previous rows, ch 4, dc in top of each of next 3 dc.* Repeat between *'s across row, ending: Dc in top of last dc, dc in top of ch 3. Ch 3, turn work.

Row 4: Same as Row 1.

Repeat from Row 1 for pattern, ending on Row 3.

GRECIAN LATTICE

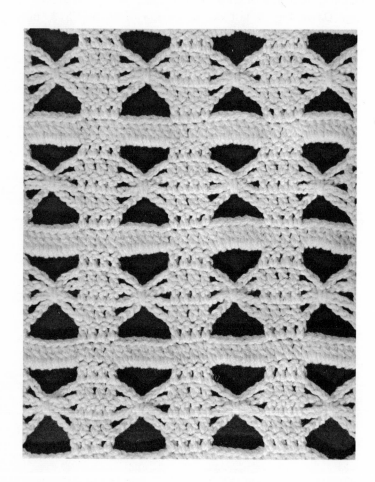

Suggested Uses: Women's vests, stoles, place setting mats, tablecloths, bedspreads, decorative panels, inserts and edgings. This pattern is equally attractive with the motifs in horizontal rows, or turned so that the motifs run in vertical stripes.

Starting Chain: Multiple of 11 plus 4. Dc in 4th ch from hook and in each ch across row. Ch 3, turn work.

Row 1: Skip first dc, dc in next dc, ch 7, skip 7 dc, *dc in each of next 4 dc, ch 7, skip 7 dc.* Repeat between *'s across row and end: Dc in last dc, dc in top of ch 3. Ch 3, turn work.

Rows 2 and 3: Skip first dc, dc in next dc, ch 7, *dc in each of next 4 dc, ch 7.* Repeat between *'s across row and end: Dc in last 2 dc. Ch 3, turn work.

Row 4: Skip first dc, dc in next dc, *ch 3, insert hook under 3rd ch 7 below hook (made on Row 1) and complete a sc, ch 3, dc in each of next 4 dc.* Repeat between *'s across row, ending last repeat: Dc in last dc, dc in top of ch 3. Ch 3, turn work.

Row 5: Same as Row 2.

Row 6: Skip first dc, dc in next dc, *7 dc through next ch 7, dc in each of next 4 dc.* Repeat between *'s across row, ending last repeat: Dc in last dc, dc in top of ch 3. Ch 3, turn work.

Repeat from Row 1 for pattern.

RAVEN'S FOOT

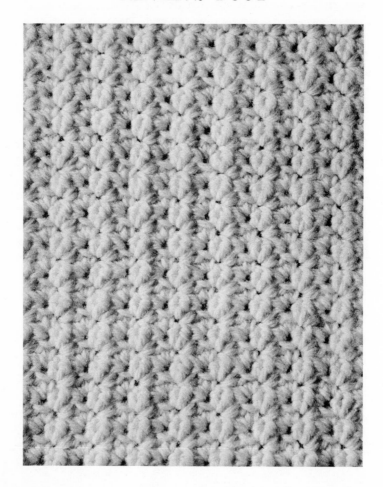

Suggested Uses: Pullovers, cardigans, vests, hats, caps, tote bags, hand bags, scatter rugs, afghans. A very attractive afghan can be made from this pattern, using dark foliage green for body of afghan, then working a border of Imperial Daisy motifs around the entire edge. (See Imperial Daisy, Part IV.)

Starting Chain: Multiple of 3. Sc in 2nd ch from hook and in each ch across row. Ch 1, turn work.
Pattern Row: Sc in first st. *Skip 2 sts, 3 sc in next st.* Repeat between *'s across row and end: Sc in last st. Ch 1, turn work.
Repeat pattern row for desired length.

WAFFLE STITCH

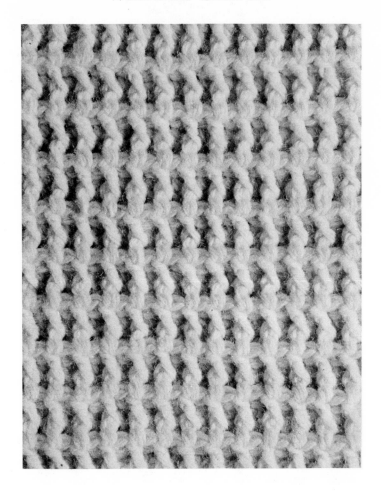

Suggested Uses: Heavy winter wear (jackets, pullovers, caps), handbags, tote bags, hot mats, upholstery fabric for footstools, hassocks, etc., decorative collars, cuffs, pockets.

Starting Chain: Even number of sts. Dc in 4th ch from hook and in each ch across row (an odd number of dc plus the ch 3 at beginning of row). Ch 3, turn work.

Pattern Row: Skip first dc, *work a dc around the post of next dc at front of work, dc in top of next dc.* Repeat between *'s across row and end: Dc in top of ch 3.

Repeat pattern row for desired length.

BLACKBERRY STITCH

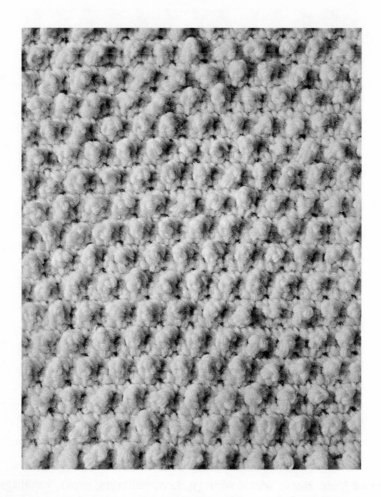

Suggested Uses: Hats, caps, tote bags, ski sweaters, jackets, scatter rugs, ornamental collars, cuffs, pockets.

Starting Chain: Even number. Sc in 2nd ch from hook and in each ch across row. Ch 1, turn work.

Row 1: Sc in first st, *draw yarn through next st, ch 3 on this loop, draw yarn through both loops on hook, sc in next st.* Repeat between *'s across row. Ch 1, turn work.

Row 2: Sc in each st across row. Ch 1, turn work.

Row 3: *Draw yarn through next st, ch 3, draw yarn through both loops on hook, sc in next st.* Repeat between *'s across row and end: Sc in last st. Ch 1, turn work.

Row 4: Same as Row 2.

Repeat from Row 1 for pattern.

ZIGZAG STITCH

Here is an old favorite which is very useful for making multicolored afghans with leftover yarns. Single-strand knitting worsted can be combined with lighter weight yarns used double strand. Use a very large hook (H, I or J) and colors as desired. A medium-size afghan requires about 48 to 52 oz of knitting worsted. If a main color is used, this will require about 36 oz, and a total of about 12 to 14 oz of several colors for the contrasting zigzag stripes. Work 4 rows of main color and 2 rows each of various contrasting colors.

Starting Chain: Multiple of 15 plus 2. Sc in 2nd ch from hook and in each ch across row. Ch 1, turn work.

Pattern Row: 2 sc in first st, *sc in each of next 6 sts, skip 2 sts, sc in each of next 6 sts, 3 sc in next st.* Repeat between *'s and end: 2 sc in last st (instead of 3).

Repeat pattern row for desired length.

MAYFAIR

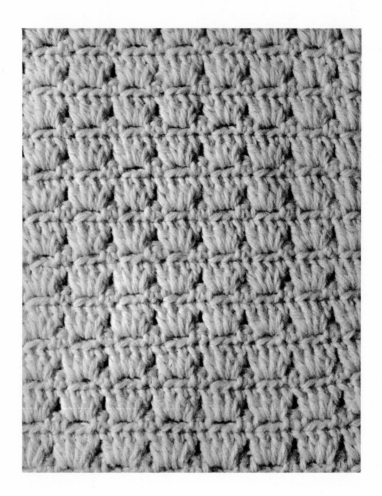

Suggested Uses: An interesting and very neutral fabric which can be used for both men's and women's wear, place setting mats, tote bags, afghans. Interesting afghans can be made by using 2 or more colors, changing each color after each Row 1 and 2 have been completed.

Starting Chain: Multiple of 4 plus 3. Sc in 2nd ch from hook and in each ch across row. Ch 1, turn work.

Row 1: Sc in each of first 2 sts, *ch 2, skip 2 sts, sc in each of next 2 sts.* Repeat between *'s across row. Ch 3, turn work.

Row 2: *4 dc in next ch 2.* Repeat between *'s across row and end: Dc in end st. Ch 1, turn work.

ACORN PUFF

Suggested Uses: Afghans, crib covers, hats, caps, handbags, tote bags, pullovers, cardigans, ornamental collars, cuffs, pockets, panels.

Starting Chain: Multiple of 4 plus 2. Sc in 2nd ch from hook and in each ch across row. Ch 2, turn work.

First Row: 3 dc in first st, *skip next 3 sts; 1 sc and 3 dc in next st.* Repeat between *'s across row, ending: Skip 3 sc, sc in last st. Ch 2, turn work.

Pattern Row: 3 dc in first st (at base of ch 2), *skip next 3 dc, 1 sc and 3 dc in next sc.* Repeat between *'s across row, ending: Sc in last st (2nd ch of previous row). Ch 2, turn work.

Repeat pattern row for desired length.

MOSS STITCH

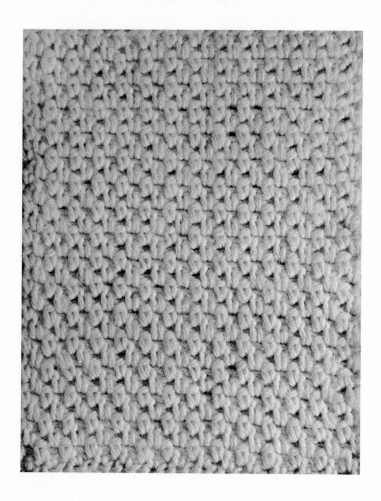

Suggested Uses: Pullovers, jackets, handbags, tote bags, slippers, hot mats, place setting mats.

Starting Chain: Odd number. Sc in 3rd ch from hook. *Ch 1, skip next ch, sc in next ch.* Repeat between *'s across row. Ch 2, turn work.
Pattern Row: Skip first sc, *sc through next ch 1, ch 1, skip next sc.* Repeat between *'s across row, ending: Sc in ch 2 of previous row. Ch 2, turn work.
Repeat pattern row for desired length.

STAR FILET

Suggested Uses: Stoles, mufflers, blouses, place setting mats, baby afghans, ornamental panels, collars, cuffs, edgings.

Starting Chain: Multiple of 5 plus 1. Sc in 2nd ch from hook and in each ch across row. Ch 4, turn work. Skip first sc, dc in next sc, *ch 1, skip next sc, dc in next sc.* Repeat between *'s across row. Ch 1, turn work.

Row 1 (reverse side): Draw yarn through first dc, through ch-1 space and through next dc, then draw yarn through all 4 loops on hook, ch 1; *draw yarn through same dc, through next ch-1 space and through next dc, then draw yarn through all 4 loops on hook, ch 1.* Repeat between *'s across row, ending: Draw yarn through same dc, through ch-4 space and through 3rd ch, then draw yarn through all 4 loops on hook. Ch 4, turn work.

Row 2: *Dc in 2 strands of st above next dc, ch 1.* Repeat between *'s across row and end: Dc in top of last dc. Ch 1, turn work.

Repeat Rows 1 and 2 for pattern.

FILIGREE

Suggested Uses: Tablecloths, place setting mats, women's vests, stoles, ornamental panels and edgings.

Starting Chain: Multiple of 4 plus 1. Sc in 2nd ch from hook and in each ch across row. Ch 6, turn work. *Skip 3 sc, dc in next sc, ch 3.* Repeat between *'s across row and end: Dc in last sc. Ch 6, turn work.

Row 1: *Sc through next ch 3, ch 2, dc in top of next dc, ch 2.* Repeat between *'s and end: Sc in ch 6, ch 2, dc in 3rd ch of ch 6, ch 6, turn work.

Row 2: *Dc in top of next dc, ch 3.* Repeat between *'s across row and end: Dc in 3rd ch of ch 6. Ch 6, turn work.

Repeat Rows 1 and 2 for pattern.

CHECKERBOARD AND CHAIN

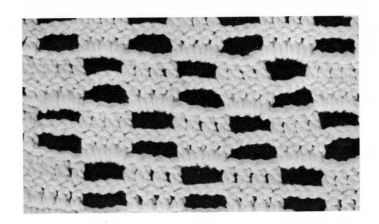

Suggested Uses: Place setting mats, mufflers, string dishcloths and shopping bags, women's vests.

Starting Chain: Multiple of 8 plus 1. Sc in 2nd ch from hook and in each ch across row. Ch. 3, turn work.

First Row: Skip first sc, dc in each of next 5 sc, *ch 4, skip 4 sc, dc in each of next 4 sc.* Repeat between *'s across row and end: Dc in each of last 2 sc. Ch 3, turn work.

Row 1: Skip first dc, dc in next 5 dc, *ch 4, skip next 4 dc, dc in next 4 dc.* Repeat between *'s across row and end: Dc in last dc, dc in top of ch 3. Ch 3, turn work.

Row 2: Skip first dc, dc in next dc, *ch 4, 4 dc through next ch-4 space.* Repeat between *'s across row and end: Ch 4, dc in last dc, dc in top of ch 3. Ch 3, turn work.

Row 3: Skip first dc, dc in next dc, *ch 4, dc in each of next 4 dc.* Repeat between *'s ending last repeat: Dc in last dc, dc in top of ch 3. Ch 3, turn work.

Row 4: Skip first dc, dc in next dc, *4 dc through next ch-4 space, ch 4.* Repeat between *'s across row and end: 4 dc through next ch-4 space, dc in last dc, dc in top of ch 3. Ch 3, turn work.

Repeat from Row 1 for pattern.

LADDER PATTERN

Suggested Uses: Place setting mats, vests, string shopping bags, mufflers. Interesting tote bags can be made with this pattern in straw yarn or heavy cotton thread. For an added decorative effect, contrasting color ribbon or cording can be woven in and out of the chain ladder sections.

Starting Chain: Multiple of 8 plus 3. Sc in 2nd ch from hook and in each ch across row. Ch 3, turn work.

First Row: Skip first sc, dc in next 2 sc, *ch 4, skip 4 sc, dc in each of next 4 sc.* Repeat between *'s, ending last repeat: Dc in last 3 sc. Ch 3, turn work.

Pattern Row: Skip first dc, dc in each of next 2 dc, *ch 4, skip next 4 dc, dc in each of next 4 dc.* Repeat between *'s across row, ending last repeat: Dc in last 2 dc, dc in top of ch 3. Ch 3, turn work.

Repeat pattern row for desired length.

PERUVIAN FILIGREE

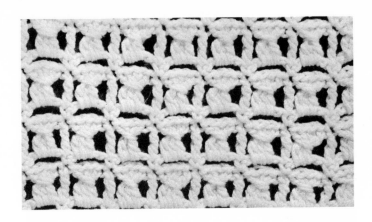

Suggested Uses: Place setting mats, tablecloths, stoles, blouses, dresses, afghans, draperies, string shopping bags, mufflers.

Starting Chain: Multiple of 4 plus 1. Sc in 2nd ch from hook and in each ch across row. Ch 4, turn work.

First Row: Skip 3 sc, sc in next sc, *ch 4, skip 3 sc, sc in next sc.* Repeat between *'s across row. Ch 4, turn work.

Row 1: *3 tr through ch 4; yarn over hook, insert hook through space at right of 3rd tr from hook, complete a dc (pulling up snugly), tr in next sc.* Repeat between *'s across row. Ch 1, turn work.

Row 2: Sc in top of tr, *ch 4, skip dc and 3 tr, sc in top of tr between motifs.* Repeat between *'s across row and end: Sc in top of ch 4. Ch 4, turn work.

Repeat Rows 1 and 2 for pattern.

DIAMOND FILET

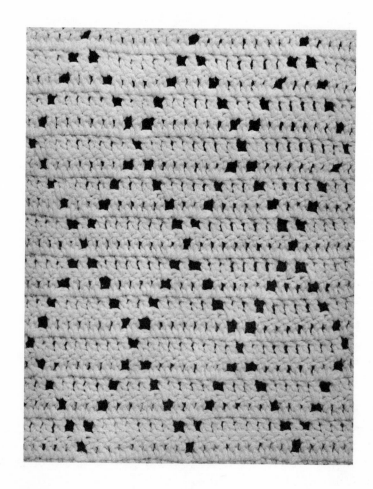

Suggested Uses: Afghans, bedspreads, place setting mats, tote bags, pullovers, cardigans, coats, decorator pillows, children's wear.

Starting Chain: Multiple of 10 plus 6. Sc in 2nd ch from hook and in each ch across row. Ch 3, turn work.

First Row: Skip first sc, dc in each of next 6 sc, *ch 1, skip next sc, dc in each of next 9 sc.* Repeat between *'s across row, ending last repeat: Dc in each of next 7 sc. Ch 3, turn work.

Row 1: Skip first dc, dc in each of next 5 dc, *ch 1, dc through ch 1 (this is a filet made on previous row), ch 1, skip next dc, dc in each of next 7 dc.* Repeat between *'s across row, ending last repeat: Dc in each of last 5 dc, dc in top of ch 3. Ch 3, turn work.

Row 2: Skip first dc, dc in each of next 4 dc, *ch 1, dc through next filet, in next dc and through next filet; ch 1, skip next dc, dc in each of next 5 dc.* Repeat between *'s across row, ending: Ch 1, skip next dc, dc in each of last 4 dc, dc in top of ch 3. Ch 3, turn work.

Row 3: Skip first dc, dc in each of next 3 dc, *ch 1, dc through next filet, in each of next 3 dc and through next filet, ch 1, skip next dc, dc in each of next 3 dc.* Repeat between *'s across row, ending: Dc in top of ch 3. Ch 3, turn work.

Row 4: Skip first dc, dc in each of next 2 dc, *ch 1, dc through next filet, in each of next 5 dc and through next filet; ch 1, skip next dc, dc in next dc.* Repeat between *'s across row, ending: Dc in last dc, dc in top of ch 3. Ch 3, turn work.

Row 5: Skip first dc, dc in next dc, *ch 1, dc through next filet, in each of next 7 dc and through next filet.* Repeat between *'s across row, ending: Ch 1, skip next dc, dc in last dc, dc in top of ch 3. Ch 3, turn work.

Row 6: Skip first dc, dc in next dc and through next filet, *ch 1, skip next dc, dc in each of next 7 dc, ch 1, through next filet.* Repeat between *'s across row, ending: Dc in last dc, dc in top of ch 3. Ch 3, turn work.

Row 7: Skip first dc, dc in each of next 2 dc and through next filet, *ch 1, skip next dc, dc in each of next 5 dc, ch 1, dc through next filet, in next dc and through next filet.* Repeat between *'s across row, ending last repeat: Dc in each of last 2 dc, dc in top of ch 3. Ch 3, turn work.

Row 8: Skip first dc, dc in each of next 3 dc and through next filet, *ch 1, skip next dc, dc in each of next 3 dc, ch 1, dc through next filet, in each of next 3 dc and through next filet.* Repeat between *'s across row, ending: Dc in top of ch 3 (instead of through filet). Ch 3, turn work.

Row 9: Skip first dc, dc in each of next 4 dc and through next filet, *ch 1, skip next dc, dc in next dc, ch 1, dc through next filet, in each of next 5 dc and through next filet.* Repeat between *'s across row, ending last repeat: Dc in each of last 4 dc, dc in top of ch 3. Ch 3, turn work.

Row 10: Skip first dc, dc in each of next 5 dc and through next filet, *ch 1, dc through next filet, in each of next 7 dc and through next filet.* Repeat between *'s across row, ending: Ch 1, dc through next filet, in each of last 5 dc, dc in top of ch 3. Ch 3, turn work.

Repeat from Row 1 for pattern.

ZIGZAG FILET

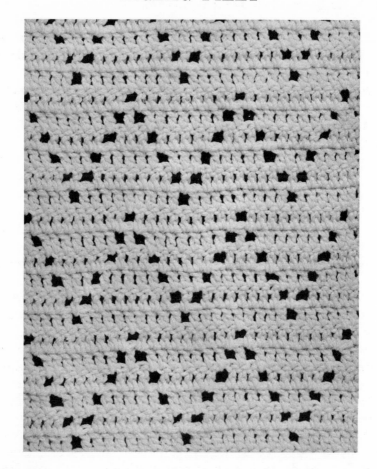

Suggested Uses: Afghans, bedspreads, place setting mats, tote bags, pullovers, cardigans, coats, decorative edgings.

Work as for Diamond Filet (see preceding pattern) from start through Row 5.

Row 6: Skip first dc, dc in next dc, through filet and in each of next 4 dc, *ch 1, skip next dc, dc in each of next 4 dc, through filet and in each of next 4 dc.* Repeat between *'s across row, ending last repeat: Dc in last dc, dc in top of ch 3. Ch 3, turn work.

Repeat from Row 1 (as directed above) for pattern.

TROIKA PATTERN

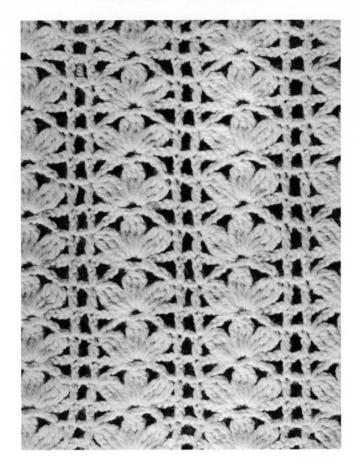

Suggested Uses: Dresses, blouses, stoles, bedspreads, tablecloths, place setting mats, decorative panels.

Starting Chain: Multiple of 12. Sc in 2nd ch from hook and in each ch across row. Ch 7, turn work.

Work a treble cluster in directions below as follows: (Yarn over hook twice, draw yarn through next ch-3 space, draw yarn through 2 strands on hook, draw yarn through next 2 strands on hook) 3 times, then draw yarn through all 4 strands on hook.

First Row: *Skip 3 sc, sc in next sc, ch 3, skip 1 sc, sc in next sc, ch 4, skip 3 sc, dc in next sc, ch 2, skip 1 sc, dc in next sc, ch 4.* Repeat between *'s across row, ending last repeat: Skip 3 sc, sc in next sc, ch 3, skip 1 sc, sc in next sc, ch 4, skip 3 sc, dc in next sc. Ch 3, turn work.

Row 1: *Work a treble cluster in next ch 3; ch 4, tr cluster in same space, ch 4, tr cluster in same space, dc in top of next dc, ch 2, dc in top of next dc.* Repeat between *'s across row, ending last repeat: Skip 3 ch, dc in 5th ch of ch 7 of previous row. Ch 7, turn work.

Row 2: *Sc through next ch 4, ch 3, sc through next ch 4; ch 4, dc in top of next dc, ch 2, dc in top of next dc, ch 4.* Repeat between *'s, ending last repeat: Dc in top of ch 3 of previous row. Ch 3, turn work. Repeat Rows 1 and 2 for pattern.

SHORT-SLEEVE DRESS OR TUNIC
in Troika Pattern

Size: Directions are given first for size 33″–34″ bust and hip measurement. Changes for larger sizes (35″–36″; 37″–38″; 39″–40″; 41″–42″) follow in parentheses.

Yarn: Lightweight dress yarn or any desired yarn yielding the stitch gauge given below. Dress sizes 33″ through 38″ require approximately 18 oz; larger sizes require approximately 22 oz. For tunic, about 2 oz less yarn is required. A very long hemline may require more yarn, and a very short hemline may require slightly less yarn than amounts given above.

Hook: Steel ✂00 (or any size required to obtain the stitch gauge given below).

Stitch Gauge: 2 patterns equal 4½".

Back and Front are identical; make 2 of the following: Beginning at upper edge, ch 108 (120, 132, 144, 156) loosely and work in Troika pattern until piece measures 7" (7", 7½", 7½", 8"), ending on Row 2 (this is the sleeve section completed). Cut yarn and fasten. Turn work and attach yarn to 2nd dc at left of first pattern motif on right-hand edge of work. Continue in pattern (beginning with Row 1) across to 2nd dc at right of last pattern motif. Ch 7, turn work and continue over these middle sts until work measures the desired tunic or dress length from shoulder seam to lower edge, ending on Row 1. Cut yarn and fasten. Sew shoulder seams, using overcast st on reverse side, and leaving a 9" opening in middle for neckline. Sew underarm and side seams. Turn right side out and work 2 rows sc around neckline, sleeves and lower edge. Block to desired measurements. A belt or chain tie can be worn at the waist, if desired.

LACY POLKA DOT

Suggested Uses: Blouses, pullovers, cardigans, stoles, coverlets, lined tote bags, decorative insertions and edgings, ornamental collars and cuffs.

Starting Chain: Multiple of 4 plus 1. Sc in 2nd ch from hook and in each chain across row. Ch 4, turn work. Skip first sc, *dc in next sc, ch 1, skip next sc.* Repeat between *'s across row and end: Dc in last sc. Ch 4, turn work.

Row 1: Holding back last loop of each tr on hook, work 4 tr in top of first dc, draw yarn through all 5 loops on hook. *Ch 3, skip next dc; holding back last loop of each tr on hook, work 5 tr in top of next dc, draw yarn through all 6 loops on hook.* Repeat between *'s across row, ending: 5-tr motif in 2nd ch of ch 4. Ch 4, turn work.

Row 2: *Dc through next ch-3 space, ch 1, dc in top of next tr motif, ch 1.* Repeat between *'s across row, omitting last ch 1. Ch 4, turn work. Repeat Rows 1 and 2 for pattern.

Part IV: A COLLECTION OF
JOINED MOTIF PATTERNS
Easy-Shape Items to Make

Design Your Own Items with
Set-Together Motifs

Small, medium and large motifs set together can be used for many decorative and practical items. Any type yarn or thread may be used, and all those leftover oddments of yarn and crochet thread can be used to create many lovely multicolored items.

Any desired motif, whether square, hexagon or round, can be utilized without the aid of a specific set of directions by simply sewing or crocheting these motifs together until the desired shape and size are obtained.

Following is a list of items which can be made very easily without instructions for these specific items. Join each motif to the last one made as it is completed until the desired shape, length and width have been reached.

Afghans
  Baby
  Pet
Bags
  Cosmetic
  Hand bags
  Shopping
  Tote
Bath mats
Bedspreads
Blouses
Covers
  Bathroom accessory
  Carriage
  Chair seat
  Couch
  Footstool and hassock
Decorative collars, cuffs, pockets
Doll clothes
Draperies
Dresses
Hair bands
Hoods
Jackets

Jumpers
Lounging robes
Mats
  Hot
  Place-setting
Mufflers
Pet basket cushions
Pet coats
Pillows (decorator)
Ponchos
Pot holders
Rugs
  Hearth
  Scatter
Scarves
Shawls (triangular)
Shrugs
Sideboard scarves
Skirts
Stoles
Tablecloths
Table runners
Upholstery fabric
Vests

OLD-FASHIONED SQUARES

Small: Using main color, ch 5, slip st to form ring.
Round 1: Ch 3, 3 dc in ring, (ch 2, 4 dc in ring) 3 times, ch 2, slip st into top of ch 3. Cut main color and fasten.
Round 2: Tie contrasting color through a ch-2 space. Ch 3, 3 dc in same space, ch 2, 4 dc in same space; (4 dc in next ch-2 space, ch 2, 4 dc in same space) 3 times. Cut contrasting color, attach main color.
Round 3: Ch 1, work a sc in top of each st and 3 sc through each ch-2 space around entire edge. Slip st into first sc. Cut main color and fasten. Sew squares together in desired shape, using overcast st on reverse side.

Medium: (2 or more colors may be combined, as desired).
Work as for small square through Round 2.

Round 3: Tie desired color through a ch-2 space. Ch 3, 3 dc in same space, ch 2, 4 dc in same space; (4 dc through next space between dc, 4 dc in next ch-2 space, ch 2, 4 dc in same space) 3 times, 4 dc through last space between dc, slip st in top of ch 3. Cut yarn, attach desired color.
Round 4: Same as Round 3 of small square. Cut yarn and fasten. Sew squares together in desired shape, using overcast st on reverse side.

Large: (2 or more colors may be combined, as desired). Work as for medium size square through Round 3.
Round 4: Cut yarn, tie desired contrasting color through a ch-2 space, ch 3, 3 dc in same space, ch 2, 4 dc in same space; (4 dc through next space between dc, 4 dc through next space between dc, 4 dc in next ch-2 space, ch 2, 4 dc in same space) 3 times, and end: 4 dc in next space between dc, 4 dc in last space between dc.
Round 5: Cut yarn, attach desired color and work the same as Round 3 of small square.

PET COAT in Old-Fashioned Squares

Size: Use small squares for small dogs and small or medium-size cats; use medium squares for medium-size dog or large cat; use large squares for large dog.

Yarn: Knitting worsted or similar; small squares, 2 oz each of 2 colors; medium squares, 3 oz each of 2 colors; large squares, 4 oz each of 2 colors. Oddments of leftover yarns can be used for a multicolor coat, using 3 or more colors, as desired.

Hook: Steel ⚔00 (or any size required to obtain the stitch gauge given below).

Stitch Gauge: Small square, 2¾" across; medium, 3½" across; large, 4½" across.

Buttons: 4; ⅝" or ¾" diameter, flat.

Make 15 squares of desired size. Using matching yarn, sew squares together as shown, on reverse side using overcast st. Sew last seam to form neckline, as illustrated in photo of finished item. Work 2 rows sc around neckline and entire outside edge of coat.

Button Tab: Ch 16, sc in 2nd ch from hook and in each ch across row. *Ch 1, turn work, sc in each st across row.* Repeat between *'s over these 15 sts until tab measures 7″ for small, 9″ for medium, 11″ for large (or desired length). Cut yarn and fasten. Sew a button to each of the 4 corners of tab, adjusting placement from narrow edges of tab to fit individual animal. Use ch-2 spaces on outer edges of squares for buttonholes in middle area of coat, as shown. Steam press lightly on reverse side or block to desired measurements.

TOTE BAG in Small Squares

Size: Approximately 12½″ square.

Yarn: Knitting worsted or similar; 4 oz main color, 4 oz contrasting color.

Hook: Steel ※0 (or any size required to obtain the stitch gauge given below) for body of tote bag, and a plastic size H or I for handle.

Stitch Gauge: Each square should measure 2½″ across.

Make 50 small squares and sew together in 2 square shapes, each containing 25 squares (5 squares wide and 5 squares long). Steam press lightly on reverse side. Work 1 row sc around each bag piece, working 3 sc in each corner. With right sides out, sew the 2 bag pieces together around 3 sides, using overcast st and matching yarn.

Handle: Using larger hook and 3 strands of yarn together, crochet a chain about 33″ long. Sew ends to inside of bag at each side, as shown.

JACKET in Medium Squares

Size: Small (34″–36″ bust), medium (38″–40″ bust), large (42″–44″ bust).

Yarn: Knitting worsted or similar; 12 oz dark color, 16 oz light color.

Hook: For body of jacket, small size, use ⚹00; medium size, F; large size, G (or any size required to obtain the stitch gauge given below); for upper portion of sleeve, use 1 size larger hook than used for jacket portion, as directed.

Stitch Gauge: On ⚹00, square should measure 3¼″ across; on size F, 3½″ across; on size G, 3¾″ across.

Make 88 medium-size squares, beginning with dark color, as shown. Sew squares together on reverse side, using overcast st, as shown in diagram. Sew squares together over shoulders, as shown in photo.

Mesh Pattern Sleeves: With right side facing, attach light color at angle of sleeve inset, and using larger size hook, work pattern across vertical edge only, as follows:

First Row: Ch 5, *skip 2 sc, dc in next dc, ch 2.* Repeat between *'s across to opposite angle of sleeve inset and end: Ch 5, turn work.

Pattern Row: *Dc in next dc, ch 2.* Repeat between *'s across row, ending: Dc in 3rd ch of ch 5. Ch 5, turn work. Repeat pattern row until sleeve measures 8″. Change to smaller hook and continue until sleeve measures 15″ (or desired length from shoulder seam to lower edge), then work 2 more rows as follows: *Dc in next dc, ch 1.* Repeat between *'s across, dc in 3rd ch of ch 5. Ch 5, turn work. (Omit last ch 5 on last row.) Cut yarn and fasten. Sew upper vertical edge of sleeve to horizontal edge of sleeve inset. Sew sleeve seam. Sew side edge of jacket. Using light color, work 1 row of sc around entire edge of jacket, working 3 sc to turn each corner on outside angles, and 3 rows (or desired number) sc around lower edge of sleeves.

Ties: Using larger hook and 2 strands of yarn together, crochet 2 chains each about 18″ long. Sew a tie to each side of upper center front of jacket, as shown. Pompons or tassels may be attached to lower ends, if desired.

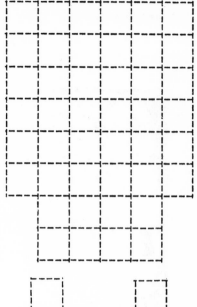

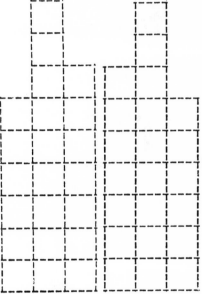

DIAGRAM A.

149

CLUSTER SQUARE

Ch 8, join with slip st to form ring.

Round 1: Ch 3; holding back last loop of each dc on hook, work 2 dc through ring and draw yarn through all 3 loops on hook (starting cluster), ch 5; holding back last loop of each dc on hook, work 3 dc through ring and draw yarn through all 4 loops on hook (a cluster made). (Ch 2, cluster in ring, ch 5, cluster in· ring) 3 times, ch 2, slip st in top of ch 3 (8 clusters in ring).

Round 2: Slip st into next ch 5, ch 3 and work a starting cluster, ch 2, cluster in same ch-5 space; ch 2, 3 dc in next ch-2 space, ch 2; *cluster, ch 2, cluster in next ch-5 space, ch 2, 3 dc in next ch-2 space, ch 2.* Repeat between *'s around to starting point. Slip st in top of ch 3.

Round 3: Slip st into next ch 2. Ch 3 and work a starting cluster, ch 2, cluster in same space; *ch 2, 2 dc in next ch-2 space, dc in top of each dc across to next ch-2 space, 2 dc in ch-2 space, ch 2; cluster, ch 2, cluster in next ch-2 space.* Repeat between *'s around 3 sides of square and end: Ch 2, 2 dc in next ch-2 space, dc in top of each dc across to next ch-2 space, 2 dc in ch-2 space, ch 2, slip st into top of ch 3.

Rounds 4 and 5: Same as Round 3.

Sew each square together on reverse side, using overcast st.

TRICOLOR FLOWER SQUARE

With flower center color, ch 7, slip st into first ch to form ring.

Round 1: Sc through ring, ch 3, 23 dc in ring. Slip st to top of ch 3 to join. Cut flower center color, attach flower petal color.

Round 2: Ch 4; holding back on hook last loop of each tr, work 2 tr in same place as slip st (at base of ch 4), draw yarn through all 3 loops on hook. *Ch 4; skip next dc; holding back on hook last loop of each tr, work 3 tr in next dc and draw yarn through all 4 loops on hook (a cluster made).* Repeat between *'s around to starting point, ch 4 and slip st in top of first cluster (a total of 12 petal clusters in circle).

Round 3: Cut petal color and fasten. Attach green to a ch-4 space. Sc through ch-4 space, *ch 5, in next ch-4 space work cluster, ch 5, cluster; (ch 5, sc in next ch-4 space) 2 times.* Repeat between *'s around to starting point. Slip st into sc to join.

Round 4: Sc in next ch-5 space, ch 3, 4 dc in same space; then work 7 dc in ch-7 space between clusters at each corner, and 5 dc in each ch-5 space across each side, around to starting point (see photo). Slip st into top of ch 3 to join. Cut yarn and fasten. Sew squares together on reverse side, using overcast st, in square set or point set, as desired.

DAISY SQUARE

Using color A, ch 5 and join with a slip st to form ring.

Round 1: *Sc in ring, ch 10.* Repeat between *'s 7 more times, slip st to first sc to join. (Total of 8 ch loops.) Cut color A and fasten.

Round 2: Attach color B to tip of a ch-10 loop. Ch 3, 2 dc in same loop, *in next loop work 3 dc, ch 3, 3 dc; 3 dc in next loop.* Repeat between *'s around, ending: 3 dc, ch 3, 3 dc in last loop. Slip st in top of ch 3 to join. Cut color B and fasten.

Round 3: Attach color C to any ch-3 corner. In same ch 3 work ch 3, 2 dc, ch 3, 3 dc; *skip 3 dc, 3 dc in next space, skip 3 dc, 3 dc in next space: in ch-3 corner, work 3 dc, ch 3, 3 dc.* Repeat between *'s around and end: 3 dc in each of next 2 spaces, slip st to top of ch 3 to join.

Round 4: Work a sc in top of each dc and 3 sc in each ch-3 corner. Slip st to first sc to join. Cut yarn and fasten.

To Join: Sew squares together on reverse side, using overcast st, in square set or point set, as desired.

152

PRIMROSE SQUARE

Round 1: With Color A, ch 5; in 4th ch from hook work 3 dc, (ch 2, 4 dc) 3 times, ch 2, slip st to top of ch to join. Break color A and fasten.
Round 2: Attach color B through a ch-2 space. Ch 3; holding back last loop of each dc, work 2 dc in same space and draw yarn through all 3 loops on hook (first cluster), ch 2, in same space, ch 4, dc in same space, ch 2; holding back last loop of each dc, work 3 dc in same space and draw yarn through all 4 loops on hook (cluster). In each of next 3 ch-2 space corners, work a cluster, ch 2, dc, ch 4, dc, ch 2, cluster. Join with a slip st to tip of first cluster.
Round 3: Ch 1, *2 sc in next ch-2 space, 5 sc in next ch-4 space, 2 sc in next ch-2 space, sc between next 2 clusters.* Repeat between *'s around to starting point and slip st to first st to join. Cut yarn and fasten.

To Join: Sew squares together on reverse side, using overcast st, in square set or point set, as desired.

IMPERIAL DAISY SQUARE

Using daisy center color, ch 5; 5 dc in 4th ch from hook; remove hook from loop, insert in top of first dc made, pull loop through, ch 1. Cut daisy center color, attach daisy petal color, ch 4, sc in base of daisy center (ch through which the 5 dc were made), ch 4, sc in ch 1 at top of daisy center so that center has a ch-4 loop on each side. Slip st into first ch-4 space.

Round 1: Ch 4; holding back on hook the last loop of each tr, work 2 tr through ch loop, then draw yarn through all 3 loops on hook (first cluster), ch 4. (Holding back on hook the last loop of each tr, work 3 tr through same ch, then draw yarn through all 4 loops on hook—a cluster made—and ch 4) 4 times. Work a cluster and ch 4 in st at base of daisy center. In ch loop on opposite side, (work a cluster, ch 4) 5 times. Work a cluster in ch 1 at top of daisy center, ch 4. Slip st into tip of first cluster made (12 petals completed). Cut yarn and fasten. Attach green.

Round 2: Sc into first ch-4 loop and work 5 sc through same space and each ch-4 loop around to starting point. Slip st to first sc to join.

Round 3: Slip st over next 2 sc; ch 5, *sc in 3rd (middle sc) of next group of 5 sc, ch 5.* Repeat between *'s around to starting point and slip st into first ch made, to join.

Round 4: Ch 3, *3 dc through next ch-5 loop, ch 2, 3 dc in same space, dc in next sc, (3 sc in next ch-5 loop, dc in next sc) 2 times.* Repeat between *'s around to starting point, and end: Omit last dc, slip st to top of ch 3 to join. Cut yarn and fasten.

To Join: Sew edges together on reverse side, using overcast st.

POPCORN FLOWER SQUARE

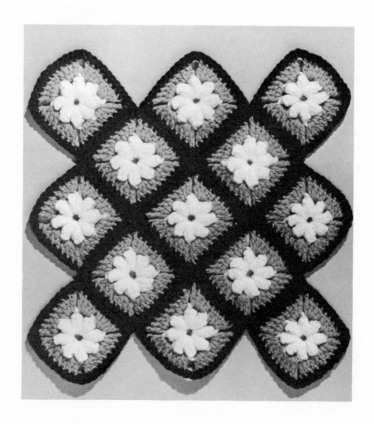

Using flower color, ch 6. Join with slip st to form ring.

Round 1: Ch 3, 4 dc in ring. Remove hook from loop, insert through top of ch 3, then pull loop through at back (first popcorn st made). *Ch 3, 5 dc in ring, remove hook from loop, insert through top of first dc made (in group of 5), then pull loop through at back (a popcorn st made).* Repeat between *'s until a total of 8 popcorn sts has been completed and end: Ch 3, slip st into top of first popcorn st to join. Cut flower color and fasten. Attach medium green (or desired color).

Round 2: Sc and ch 3 through ch 3 of Round 1; 3 dc in same ch, *ch 3, 4 dc in next ch 3, 4 dc in next ch 3.* Repeat between *'s around to starting point, ending last repeat: Ch 3, 4 dc in last ch 3, slip st into top of ch 3 to join. Cut medium green and fasten. Attach dark green (or desired color).

Round 3: Sc in top of ch 3, sc in top of each dc and 3 sc through each ch 3 at corners around to starting point. Slip st to join.

To Join: Sew squares together on reverse side, using overcast st in matching yarn, in point set or square set, as desired.

LACY POPCORN FLOWER SQUARE

Using flower color, ch 6. Join with slip st to form ring.

Round 1: Ch 3, 4 dc in ring. Remove hook from loop, insert through top of ch 3, then pull loop through at back (first popcorn st made). *Ch 3, 5 dc in ring, remove hook from loop, insert through top of first dc made (in group of 5), then pull loop through at back (a popcorn st made).* Repeat between *'s until a total of 8 popcorn sts has been made, and end: Ch 3, slip st into top of first popcorn st to join. Cut flower color and fasten. Attach green.

Round 2: Sc and ch 3 through ch 3 of Round 1; 3 dc in same ch, *ch 3, 4 dc in next ch 3, 4 dc in next ch 3.* Repeat between *'s around to starting point, ending last repeat: Ch 3, 4 dc in last ch 3, slip st into top of ch 3 to join. Cut green and fasten.

158

Round 3: Attach white (or desired contrasting color) through a ch-3 space. Sc and ch 3, 2 dc through same space, ch 2, 3 dc through same space, *ch 2, skip 2 dc, dc between 2nd and 3rd dc (of next group of 4 dc), ch 2, skip 2 dc, dc in next space (between the 2 groups of 4 dc), ch 2, skip 2 dc, dc between 2nd and 3rd dc of next group, ch 2; in next ch-3 space work 3 dc, ch 2, 3 dc (a shell made).* Repeat between *'s around, ending last repeat: Omit last shell of last repeat and join last ch 2 with a slip st into top of ch 3 of corner shell.

Rounds 4, 5 and 6: Slip st across 2 dc and into ch-2 space. Ch 3, 2 dc in same space, ch 2, 3 dc in same space, ch 2, *(dc in next ch-2 space, ch 2) across to corner shell, work a shell in ch-2 space of shell, ch 2.* Repeat between *'s around, ending last repeat: Omit last shell of last repeat and slip st into top of ch 3 to join.

Round 7: Slip st across 2 dc and into ch-2 space; ch 3, 2 dc, ch 2, 3 dc in same space, ch 2, *(skip next ch-2 space, shell in next ch-2 spaces) 3 times, ch 2, shell in ch-2 space of corner shell, ch 2.* Repeat between *'s around, ending last repeat: Omit last corner shell and last ch 2 of last repeat and slip st into top of ch 3 to join.

Second and all subsequent squares: Work Rounds 1 through 6 and join squares on Round 7 as follows: Place completed square at right and join by working half a shell (3 dc and ch 1), beginning at a corner, sc through ch 2 of corner shell of completed square, then complete shell with 3 dc. Join each shell in the same manner across one or more sides of completed squares, as required, making sure that each edge shell is joined to the corresponding edge shell of completed square, as shown, and completing open edges of square as for first square.

LIANDRA LACE

First Motif: Ch 6, join with slip st to form ring.

Round 1: Ch 3, 2 dc in ring, ch 3, (3 dc in ring, ch 3) 3 times, slip st into top of ch 3 to join.

Round 2: Ch 3, dc in same place, dc in top of next dc, 2 dc in top of next dc, ch 5, (2 dc in top of next dc, dc in top of next dc, 2 dc in top of next dc, ch 5) 3 times. Slip st in top of ch 3 to join.

Round 3: Ch 3, dc in same place, dc in top of next dc, ch 2, skip next dc, dc in top of next dc, 2 dc in top of next dc. (Ch 2, dc in next ch, ch 2, dc in same ch, ch 2, 2 dc in top of next dc, dc in top of next dc, ch 2, skip next dc, dc in top of next dc, 2 dc in top of next dc) 3 times, and end: Ch 2, dc in next ch, ch 2, dc in same ch, ch 2, slip st to top of ch 3 to join. Cut yarn and fasten.

First Row: Join 2nd and all succeeding motifs as follows: Work Rounds 1 and 2. On 3rd round, and with completed motif at right, work to first parenthesis, ch 2, dc in ch, ch 1, sc through corresponding ch of completed motif, dc in same ch, ch 2, 2 dc in top of next dc, dc in next dc, ch 1, sc through corresponding ch 2 of completed motif, skip next dc, dc in top of next dc, 2 dc in top of next dc, ch 2, dc in next ch, ch 1, sc through corresponding ch 2 of completed motif, and finish Round 3 per directions. Continue to join each succeeding motif in this manner until strip is of desired width.

Second and all succeeding rows: Join first motif of 2nd row at first 2 joining points (as for first row); join at 3rd point with a sc through sc of previously joined corner. Join 2nd and all succeeding motifs at proper joining points along 2 sides, beginning at upper right corner of completed motif, as shown in photo.

MALTESE CROSS

Work as for Liandra Lace (preceding pattern) through Round 2. Slip st to top of ch 3 to join. Cut yarn and fasten. Join at corners, as shown, with ch 3, sc through completed motif, ch 2. Join squares at one or more sides, as required. When a square is to be joined to a previously joined corner, join with a sc over all previous sc joinings and through ch on opposite side (see photo).

LACY DAHLIA

First Square: Ch 9, join with slip st to form ring.

Round 1: Ch 1, 24 sc in ring. Slip st in first sc to join.

Round 2: Ch 4; holding back on hook last loop of each tr, work 2 tr in same place as slip st (at base of ch 4), draw yarn through all 3 loops on hook. *Ch 4, skip next sc; holding back on hook last loop of each tr, work 3 tr in next sc and draw yarn through all 4 loops on hook (a cluster made).* Repeat between *'s around to starting point, ch 4 and slip st to top of first cluster (total of 12 petal clusters in circle).

Round 3: Slip st into next 2 ch, sc through ch-4 space, *ch 5; in next ch-4 space work cluster, ch 5, cluster; (ch 5, sc in next ch-4 space) 2 times.* Repeat between *'s around to starting point. Slip st into sc to join. Cut yarn and fasten.

First Row: Work 2nd and all succeeding squares in first row through Round 2 and join as follows: Work ch 5 and first cluster, ch 3; with completed square at right, sc through ch 5 between clusters of completed square, ch 2, cluster in same ch 4, ch 3, sc through next ch 5 of completed square, ch 2, sc through next ch 4, ch 3, sc through next ch 5 of completed square, ch 2, sc through next ch 4, ch 3, sc through next ch 5 of completed square, ch 2, cluster and ch 3 through next ch 4, sc through ch between clusters of completed square, ch 2, cluster in same ch 4 and complete Round 3 per directions. Continue joining each square of first row to desired width.

Second and all succeeding rows: Join squares on one or more sides, as required, in the same manner. When a square is to be joined to a previously joined corner, join with a sc over all previous sc joinings. See photo.

LACY POPCORN SQUARE

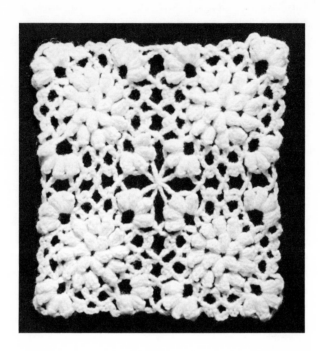

First Square: Ch 6, slip st to form ring.

Round 1: Ch 3, 4 dc in ring, drop loop from hook and insert in top of ch 3, pull loop through (first popcorn st made), *ch 3, 5 dc in ring, drop loop from hook and insert in top of first dc made, pull loop through (a popcorn st made).* Repeat between *'s 4 more times and end: Ch 3, slip st into top of first popcorn st to join; (6 popcorn sts in ring).

Round 2: Slip st into ch-3 space, ch 3, 4 dc in same space and complete first popcorn st (as in Round 1), ch 3, work a 5-dc popcorn st in same space, *ch 3; in next space work 2 popcorn sts with a ch 3 between.* Repeat between *'s 4 more times and end: Ch 3, slip st into top of first popcorn st to join; (12 popcorn sts around, with ch 3 between).

Round 3: Slip st into ch-3 space, ch 8, dc in same space; *in next ch-3 space work 1 dc, ch 5, 1 dc.* Repeat between *'s around to starting point; slip st into 3rd ch of ch 8 to join.

Round 4: Slip st into ch-5 space; ch 3, 4 dc in same space and complete first popcorn, ch 3, popcorn st in same space, ch 6, 2 popcorn sts with ch 3 between in same space (corner made), *ch 5, sc in next space, ch 3, sc in same space, ch 5, sc in next space, ch 3, sc in same space, ch 5; in next space work 2 popcorn sts with ch 3 between, ch 6, 2 popcorn sts with ch 3 between in same space.* Repeat between *'s 2 more times and end: Ch 5, sc in next space, ch 3, sc in same space, ch 5, sc in next space, ch 3, sc in same space, ch 5, slip st into top of first popcorn st to join. Cut yarn and fasten.

To Join 2nd Square: Work through Round 3 and join on last round as follows: Slip st into space, ch 3, 4 dc and complete first popcorn st, ch 3, popcorn st in same space, ch 3, sc in corner space of first square, ch 3; in same space, work popcorn st, ch 3, popcorn st; ch 2, skip next ch-3 loop of first square, sc in next space of first square, ch 2, sc in next space of 2nd square, ch 3, sc in same space, ch 2, sc in next ch-5 loop of first square, ch 2, sc in next space of 2nd square, ch 3, sc in same space, ch 2, sc in next ch-5 space of first square, ch 2; in next space work 2 popcorn sts with ch 3 between, ch 3, sc in corner space of first square, ch 3; in same space work 2 popcorn sts with ch 3 between, complete 2nd square as for first. Join each square together in the same manner on as many sides as are necessary on each row. When joining a square to a previously joined corner, sc over the sc already joining the attached squares, as shown in photo.

JONQUIL MEDALLION

The joined medallions in photo were worked with knitting worsted, using a size F hook for petal section and a ⚹0 hook for the trumpet. For other weights of yarn and crochet cotton, use a hook 2 sizes smaller for the trumpet than the hook used for the petal section. Suggested uses: Lined pillows and tote bags, decorative edgings, borders and panels, bedspreads, stoles.

Petal Medallion: Using yellow yarn and larger size hook, ch 7 and slip st in first ch to form ring. Ch 6, *wrap yarn around hook 3 times, insert through ring and draw yarn through, (yarn over hook, draw through 2 loops on hook) 3 times.* Work between *'s 3 times, then draw yarn through all 4 loops on hook (first petal made). *Ch 7, **wrap yarn around hook 3 times, insert through ring and draw yarn through, (yarn over hook, draw

167

through 2 loops on hook) 3 times.** Work between **'s 4 times, then draw yarn through all 5 loops on hook (a petal made).* Work between *'s 5 times, to total 6 petals in ring, with a ch 7 between; ch 7, slip st into top of first petal to join. Cut yellow yarn and fasten. Tie dark green yarn to cut strand. Work 9 sc through each ch-7 space around to starting point (see photo). Slip st into first sc made. Cut dark green and fasten.

Trumpet: Using orange or coral yarn and smaller size hook, make a slip loop about 12″ from cut end of yarn; ch 5 (at skein end of yarn), then work 14 dc in 4th ch from hook, to form a cup-shaped circle of dc sts (see photo). Slip st into top of ch 5 to join. Cut yarn about 12″ from hook and pull through loop. With hook, pull this cut end strand through st strands along outer side of trumpet and tie both end strands in a firm double knot. Thread both of these strands through a large yarn needle and pull through center of petal medallion. Sew base of trumpet firmly to center of petal medallion at underside. Fasten securely, draw yarn through 2 or 3 st strands at underside and cut yarn close to fabric.

To Join Medallions: Sew together at 4th, 5th and 6th (3 middle) sc between petals on reverse side, using dark green yarn and overcast st through outside strands of each sc. Set first row together at opposite sides to use for single panels, edgings and inserts. Set all succeeding rows at one or more sections as necessary. See photo.

AFGHAN with Jonquil Medallion Trim
(Not illustrated)

Size: Approximately 48"×65".

Yarn: Knitting worsted; 48 oz dark green, 4 oz pale yellow, 3 oz orange.

Hook: For body of afghan use size I; for jonquil medallion base use size F; for jonquil trumpet use ⚹0.

Using dark green and I hook, ch 168 and work in Raven's Foot pattern (Part III) until piece measures about 58" long. Cut yarn and fasten. Work Jonquil Medallions, as needed, and using hook sizes above. Use pale yellow yarn for petals, orange for trumpet and dark green for outside edge. Sew together in single strips to match length and width of body of afghan, and sew to outside edges of afghan as border.
Steam press body of afghan lightly on reverse side.

FLOWER LACE

First Motif: Ch 6, join with slip st to form ring.

Round 1: Ch 4 (yarn over hook twice, draw yarn through ring and through 2 strands on hook, yarn over and draw through 2 strands on hook) 3 times, a total of 4 loops on hook, then draw yarn through all 4 loops on hook, ch 5, *work a treble cluster as follows: Repeat directions in parentheses above 4 times, draw yarn through all 5 loops on hook, ch 5.* Repeat between *'s 5 times. Join with a slip st in top of first petal made (a total of 6 petals in ring). Cut yarn and fasten.

Join 2nd and all motifs of first row as follows: Work first petal of Round 1, ch 3, sc through a ch-5 space of completed motif, ch 2, complete 2nd (and all following) motifs as for first. Continue joining motifs in this manner until first row of fabric is of desired width or length, joining each succeeding motif to ch 5 directly opposite previous joining point.

Join 2nd and all succeeding motif rows as follows: Working from left to right, join first and last motifs in even-numbered rows at 2 joining points, and all motifs in between at 3 joining points. Join first motif in odd-numbered rows at 1 joining point and balance where necessary, until fabric is of desired width or length. Motifs may also be joined together in various shapes, such as round or triangular, by joining as desired.

STAR FLOWER LACE

This pattern adapts itself well to round shapes. A particularly lovely round tablecloth can be made by using mercerized cotton crochet thread, size 10 or 20, in a desired flower color and a foliage green. Use a size 2 or 3 hook (or any size hook which will comfortably accommodate thread being used). Start the cloth by setting motifs together in rows of 2, 3 and 2 (as shown in photo), then joining all succeeding motifs around outside circular edge until desired diameter has been reached. Use oddments of leftover crochet thread to make small doilies, place setting mats, coasters.

First Motif: With flower color, ch 6.

Round 1: In 5th ch from hook, and holding back last loop of each tr on hook, work 2 tr; draw yarn through all 3 loops on hook, ch 5. In same ch, (holding back last loop of each tr on hook, work 3 tr and draw yarn through all 4 loops on hook, ch 5) 5 times, to total 6 petals in same ch. Slip st last ch 5 to tip of first petal to join. Cut flower color and fasten. Attach green at same place.

Round 2: 7 sc through first ch-5 space and in each ch-5 space around to starting point. Slip st to first sc to join.

Round 3: *Ch 6, sc in 4th (middle) sc between next 2 petals, ch 6, sc between sc at tip of next petal.* Repeat between *'s around to starting point, and end: Slip st last ch 6 to sc at tip of petal. Cut yarn and fasten.

Second and all succeeding motifs in first row: Work first 2 rounds as above and join on Round 3 as follows: Ch 3, sc through a ch-6 space on completed motif, ch 2, sc through middle sc between next 2 petals, ch 3, sc through next ch-6 space at right, on completed motif; ch 2, sc through tip of next petal. Complete motif per directions in Round 3. Attach next motif in the same manner to each of the 2 ch-6 loops on opposite side until strip is of desired width.

Second and all succeeding rows: Join ch loops in pairs at as many points as necessary, as shown.

EMBOSSED FLORAL MEDALLION

First Medallion: Ch 6, join with slip st to form ring.

Round 1: Ch 3, 3 dc in ring. Remove hook from loop, insert through top of ch 3, then pull loop through at back (first popcorn st made). *Ch 3, 4 dc in ring, remove hook from loop, insert through top of first dc made (in group of 4), then pull loop through at back (popcorn st made).* Repeat between *'s until a total of 6 popcorn sts has been completed; ch 3, slip st into top of first popcorn st made.

Round 2: Slip st through ch-3 loop of previous round, ch 3, (yarn over hook, draw yarn through ch, draw yarn through 2 loops on hook) 3 times, then draw yarn through all 5 loops on hook (first petal made). *Ch 6, repeat directions in parentheses above through next ch-3 space 4 times, draw yarn through all 5 loops on hook (petal made).* Repeat between *'s until a total of 6 petals has been completed; ch 6, slip st into top of first petal made.

Round 3: Ch 1, *7 sc through next ch 6 of previous round.* Repeat between *'s around to starting point and slip st into ch 1. Cut yarn and fasten. Join 2nd and all succeeding medallions in first row as follows: Work Rounds 1 and 2 as for first medallion; 3 sc through ch 6, sc through 4th sc of a Round 3 section of first medallion, 3 sc through same ch 6 and complete as for first medallion. Continue joining medallions in this manner on first row, joining each succeeding medallion to section directly opposite previous joining point, as shown.

Second and all succeeding medallion rows: Working from left to right, join first and last medallions in even-numbered rows at 2 joining points, and all medallions in between at 3 joining points; join first medallion in odd-numbered rows at 1 joining point, and all succeeding medallions at 3 joining points. Medallions may also be set together in triangular, circular or desired shape.

TWELVE-PETAL DAISY MOTIF

Suggested Uses: Tablecloths, bedspreads, place setting mats, draperies, doilies. Attractive dresses and blouses can be made from this pattern, using baby wool or lightweight dress yarn, lined with jersey of contrasting color.

Motif: Ch 8, slip st in first ch to form ring.
Round 1: Ch 3, 23 dc through ring, join with slip st in top of ch 3.
Round 2: Ch 10, sc in 4th ch from hook, hdc in next ch, dc in each of next 3 ch; skip next dc in Round 1, dc in next dc, *ch 8, sc in 4th ch from hook, hdc in next ch, dc in each of next 3 ch, skip next dc in Round 1, dc in next dc.* Repeat between *'s around to starting point, ending last repeat: Slip st into 3rd ch of ch 10 (12 petals made). Cut yarn and fasten.

Joined Motif: Work as for first motif, joining 2 petals at a time, as follows: On first petal ch 8 (instead of 10), sc in tip of petal of completed motif, counting as 1 ch; ch 1, then complete petal as in Round 2 above. On each succeeding petal, ch 6, sc in tip of corresponding petal of completed motif, counting as 1 ch; ch 1, then complete petal and balance of motif as in Round 2. Set each motif together, as shown, in as many points as necessary on each row.

HEXAGON FLOWER MOTIF

First Motif: Using flower color, ch 6, join with slip st to form ring.

Round 1: *Ch 3, 3 dc in ring, ch 3, sc in ring.* Repeat between *'s 5 more times (a total of 6 petals around ring). Cut flower color, attach green.

Round 2: Sc through ring over sc (between petals), *ch 4, sc through ring over next sc, keeping ch 4 behind petal.* Repeat between *'s around and end: Ch 4, slip st in first sc made.

Round 3: Slip st into ch 4, ch 3, 2 dc in ch 4, ch 2, 3 dc in same ch 4, *3 dc in next ch 4, ch 2, 3 dc in same ch 4.* Repeat between *'s around. Slip st in top of ch 3 to join. Cut yarn and fasten.

Second Motif: Work as above through Round 2. Join 2nd and all succeeding motifs together on Round 3, as follows: (slip st into ch 4, ch 3,

2 dc in ch 4, ch 1, slip st through ch 2 of completed motif, ch 1, 3 dc in same ch 4, *3 dc in next ch 4, ch 1, slip st through ch 2 of completed motif at the right of previous joining, ch 1, 3 dc in same ch 4*). Work directions in parentheses, repeating between *'s as necessary, at joining points only, and complete unjoined edges as for first motif. Where a motif must be joined at a point where it is already joined to another motif, slip st through completed joining slip st. Always join motifs from right to left. See photo.

LACY FLOWER MOTIF

First Motif: Using flower color, ch 6, join with slip st to form ring.

Round 1: *Ch 3, 3 dc in ring, ch 3, sc in ring.* Repeat between *'s 5 more times (a total of 6 petals around ring). Cut flower color, attach green (or desired color).

Round 2: Sc through ring over sc (between petals), *ch 4, sc through ring over next sc, keeping ch 4 behind petal.* Repeat between *'s around and end: Ch 4, slip st in first sc made.

Round 3: *Ch 5, sc through next ch, ch 5, sc in next sc.* Repeat between *'s around to starting point, ending last repeat: Slip st in sc (12 ch-5 loops).

Second Motif: Work as above through Round 2. Join second and all succeeding motifs on Round 3 as follows: Ch 2, sc through a ch-4 loop of first motif, ch 2, sc through next ch 4 of 2nd motif, ch 2, sc in next ch 4 at the right, ch 2, sc in next sc of 2nd motif. Complete as for first motif. Each joining point should be connected by 2 ch-5 loops. Set motifs together with 1 joining point (2 loops) on first row. On succeeding rows, join each motif at as many joining points as necessary, always joining from left to right. See photo.

OCTAGON AND SQUARE

This pattern makes very interesting place setting mats. Use bedspread cotton either single strand, or 2 strands together for faster completion, and any steel crochet hook which will comfortably accommodate the thread. Size of place setting mats varies from about 12″ to 14″ wide and 16″ to 18″ long. Set the motifs together until mat is of desired size, with the octagon motifs around all outside edges. No finishing edge is necessary. The small squares connecting the octagon motifs can be of a contrasting color, if desired.

First Octagon: Ch 7, slip st in first ch to form ring.

Round 1: Ch 4, tr in ring, ch 3, *2 tr in ring, ch 3.* Repeat between *'s 6 more times and slip st into top of ch 4 to join. There will now be a total of 8 pairs of tr in ring (counting first ch 4 as a tr) with a ch 3 between each pair.

182

Round 2: Slip st into top of next tr and into ch 3. In this ch-3 space, ch 4, 2 tr, ch 2, 3 tr. In each remaining ch-3 space, work 3 tr, ch 2, 3 tr. Slip st into top of ch 4 at starting point to join.

Join 2nd and all subsequent octagons in first row as follows: Work Round 1 as for first octagon. Work into first ch-3 space of Round 2 as directed. Place completed motif at right and join by working 3 tr and ch 1, sc through a ch-2 space of completed motif, 3 tr in same space of motif being joined. Join same motif at next ch-2 space. (See first row in photo.) Continue joining octagon motifs in this manner at 2 joining points directly opposite the previously joined point on first row, as shown, until desired width or length has been completed.

Square Motif Row: Ch 7, join with slip st to form ring. Ch 4, 5 tr in ring, ch 1, sc in upper right ch-2 space of octagon, 6 tr in ring, ch 1, sc through sc joining next octagon, 6 tr in ring, ch 1, sc through ch-2 space at right on next octagon (see photo), 6 tr in ring, ch 2, slip st to top of ch 4 to join. Work a square motif and join between each 2 octagons in the same manner across row, as shown.

Next Octagon Row: Join first octagon motif at first ch-2 space at upper edge, through sc space where octagon and square have been joined, and at upper tip of square. Join second and all subsequent octagons as follows: Join at ch-2 space at right above square motif, through sc joining octagon and square of previous row directly below, through next sc joining octagon and square, through next sc joining octagon and square, and in ch-2 space at upper point of square, totaling 5 joining points. Join last octagon of each row at 4 joining points, as shown. Complete all unjoined edges of octagons as directed in Round 2. Alternate a square motif row and an octagon motif row for desired width or length.

TWO-COLOR BOWS

Suggested Uses: Pullovers, blouses, afghans. An interesting afghan can be made by working light color on one side to half the desired length, then changing to dark color for the balance of the length. On the opposite side, work dark color for the first half of desired length, then change to light color for balance of the length. Use a large hook, size H or I, and knitting worsted. An afghan of medium size requires about 36 oz of each of two colors. For a light- and dark-striped afghan with the inside strips having chain loops on both edges, repeat Row 1 only for desired length, omitting the ch-2 turning chain.

Starting Chain: Any desired number. Hdc in 3rd ch from hook and in each ch across row. Continue to Row 1 before turning work.

Row 1: Make a ch measuring 3¼" long and turn work. Hdc at base of ch, in each st across row and in top of turning ch (last st). Ch 2, turn work.

Row 2: Hdc in each st across row.

Repeat these 2 rows, making sure that each row contains the same number of sts and that each ch loop contains the same number of ch sts. Work 2 pieces each of the same length, using contrasting colors as desired.

Tie Chain Loops: Place loop edges of fabric together and tie corresponding loops together with a firm double knot; on second knot, pull each loop toward the contrasting color fabric, as illustrated.

TREBLE SHELL

Suggested Uses: Afghans, bedspreads, stoles, scarves, dresses, blouses, women's vests, draperies.

First Strip: Ch 10, slip st to form ring. Ch 4, 4 tr in ring, ch 5, 5 tr in ring. *Ch 10, but do not turn work; sc in ch 5 (between tr groups), ch 4, 4 tr through both chains, ch 5, 5 tr through both chains.* Repeat between *'s until strip is of desired length and end: Ch 5, slip st in 5th tr from left. Cut yarn and fasten.

Joined Strips: Using contrasting color, ch 10, slip st to form ring. Ch 4, 4 tr in ring, ch 5, 5 tr in ring, sc through ch 4 at edge of first shell of previous strip. *Ch 10, but do not turn work; sc in ch 5 (between tr groups), ch 4, 4 tr through both chains, ch 5, 5 tr through both chains, sc through ch 4 of next shell of previous strip.* (See photo.) Repeat between *'s until the same number of shells has been completed as in previous strip (count each shell in each strip as it is completed to make sure each strip contains the exact number as previous strip), and end: Ch 5, slip st into top of 5th tr from left. Cut yarn and fasten. Continue working joined strips until fabric is of desired width.

POPOVER TOP in Treble Shell Pattern

Size: Directions are given first for size 34"–36" bust measurement. Changes for larger sizes (38"–40", 42"–44") follow in parentheses.

Yarn: Knitting worsted; 12 oz light color and 12 oz dark color are required for size 34–36; sizes 38–40 and 42–44 requires 16 oz each color.

Hook: Steel ⚹0 (or any size required to obtain the stitch gauge given below).

Stitch Gauge: 3 shells in vertical strip measures 3"; 1 shell measures 2" across.

Front and Back are identical; make 2 of the following: Starting at upper edge of garment and at vertical edge of left sleeve, work first Treble Shell strip in dark color with 7 (8, 8) shells. Attach joined strips, alternating light and dark colors and continuing to work the same number of shells, until 6 strips have been completed. Beginning body of garment, continue working strips of dark and light color, as follows: Attach first shells in first body strip to shells of sleeve strip, then continue working as for starting strip until a total of 26 shells has been completed. Attach strips of 26 shells to each previous strip until body of garment contains 9 (11, 13) strips, beginning and ending with a dark strip. Work second sleeve section the same as for first: 6 strips containing 7 (8, 8) shells, beginning with light color and ending with dark color.

Side Strips (used for joining front and back together); make 2: Using light color, work a single strip containing 20 (19, 19) shells. Join sides: Place a side strip on vertical edge of one side of garment, with right sides together and shells facing the same direction. With yarn needle and light color, sew shell strip to garment body, attaching sewing yarn at lower edge. Sew side tips of shells together with a firm overcast st through top of both edge sts, then slide needle through underside sts of light strip only, downward from overcast st, then upward through underside sts of next shell; join next shell through top sts. Continue joining in this manner to end of side strip. Place unjoined edge of side strip along vertical edge of other side of garment and sew the same. Sew second side strip on opposite side.

Join underside of sleeve seams as follows: With right side out, attach light color through middle ch of uppermost shell of side strip just sewn. Ch 4, sc through middle ch of light color shell at right, tr through ch of side strip shell, ch 2, 2 tr through same ch, sc through middle ch of light color shell at left, ch 4, do not turn work; sc through ch 2, ch 4, sc between light and dark sleeve shells at right, 3 tr through same ch 2, sc between light and dark sleeve shells at left. Cut yarn and fasten. Turn garment inside out and place lower sleeve edges together. Attach dark yarn through ch 5 of both of first dark color shells; 5 sc through both ch-5 spaces, (ch 6, 5 sc through both ch-5 spaces) 4 times. Cut yarn and fasten. Join corresponding underside sleeve seam the same. Join upper sleeve seams the same, working directions in parentheses above until a total of 8 (9, 10) shoulder strips has been joined each side, leaving an opening in middle for neckline. **Neckline edge:** With right side out, attach dark yarn between light and dark shells at right side of neckline (ch 5, 5 sc in middle ch of next shell, ch 5, sc through space between shells) 5 times; sc through space between next light and dark shells, then repeat direction in parentheses again 5 times along edge of neckline on opposite side; sc through space between next light and dark shells. Cut yarn and fasten. Steam press lightly on reverse side, or block to desired measurements.

TRITON SHELL

Suggested Uses: Afghans, bedspreads, draperies, blouses, cardigans, pull-overs, ornamental panels. Very attractive 2-piece stoles can be made from this interesting pattern by working 2 sections of desired width and each measuring half the desired length; sew or crochet the lower chain edges together at center back. (See page headed STOLES, page 209.) The photo shows the pattern in 2 colors; however, oddments of leftover yarn may be used to create multicolor items.

First Strip: Ch 8, slip st to form ring. Ch 3, 7 dc through ring. *Ch 5, but do not turn work; instead, sc in top of 4th dc from left edge. Ch 3, 7 dc through ch 5 just made.* Repeat between *'s until strip is of desired length. Cut yarn and fasten.

Joined Strips: Using contrasting color, ch 4, sc through ch 3 at edge of first shell made on previous strip, ch 4, slip st in first ch to form ring. Ch 3, 7 dc through ring. *Sc through ch 3 of next shell of previous strip. Ch 5, but do not turn work; instead, sc in top of 4th dc from left edge. Ch 3, 7 dc through ch 5 just made.* (See photo.) Repeat between *'s until the same number of shells has been completed as in previous strip (count each shell in each strip as it is completed to make sure each strip contains the exact number as previous strip), and end: Slip st into top of 2nd dc of last shell of previous strip. Cut yarn and fasten. Continue working joined strips until fabric is of desired width.

CARDIGAN in Triton Shell Pattern

Size: Directions are given first for small (34″–36″ bust measurements). Changes for larger sizes (medium, 38″–40″; large, 42″–44″) follow in parentheses.

Yarn: Knitting worsted; small, 16 oz light color and 16 oz dark color; medium, 18 oz each color; large, 20 oz each color.

Hook: If crochet is done loosely, use steel ⋇00; if crochet is done snugly, use aluminum size F (or any size required to obtain the stitch gauge given below).

Stitch Gauge: 2 joined strips measure 2½" wide; 5 shells measure 4" long.

Buttons: ¾" to ⅞" diameter, 9.

Back: Work 2 (3, 3) strips each containing 28 shells, beginning with dark color and alternating strips of light and dark, as shown. On 3rd (4th, 4th) strip, continue working as for starting strip (after 28th shell) until 37 (38, 38) shells have been completed. Add joined strips of 37 (38, 38) shells across back, alternating colors, until a total of 13 (14, 16) strips has been completed from start. Work 2 (3, 3) more strips, each containing 28 shells each, to total 15 (17, 19) strips across back, including shorter sleeve-inset strips on each side.

Right Front: Work 2 (3, 3) strips each containing 28 shells, beginning with light color and alternating strips of dark and light, as shown. On 3rd (4th, 4th) strip, continue working as for single strip until 37 (38, 38) shells have been completed. Add joined strips of 37 (38, 38) shells until a total of 5 (6, 7) strips has been completed from start. **Shape neckline:** On 6th (7th, 8th) strip, work 34 (35, 35) shells. Work another strip of 34 (35, 35) shells to complete neckline, and to total 7 (8, 9) strips across right front.

Left Front: Work strips in opposite order to correspond with right front, as follows: Using the same color yarn for first strip as was used for last strip on right front, work first 2 strips with 34 (35, 35) shells for neckline; next 3 (3, 4) strips with 37 (38, 38) shells for shoulder area; next 2 (3, 3) strips with 28 shells each for sleeve inset, to total 7 (8, 9) strips across left front.

Sleeves: Work 12 (14, 14) strips of 21 shells each, alternating colors. Sew shoulder seams on reverse side. Pin upper horizontal edge of sleeve on reverse side to vertical edge of sleeve inset, between angles of horizontal edges, and sew. Sew upper vertical edges of sleeve to horizontal edges of sleeve insets. Sew remaining vertical edges of sleeve seams and side seams.

Button Edge: Attach matching color yarn at upper edge of left center front edge. Work a row of sc down this edge, working 2 sc through each edge dc and through space between each motif. Ch 1, turn work, then work 1 more row of sc along this edge. Cut matching yarn, attach contrasting color yarn, and work 7 more rows sc along this edge.

Buttonhole Edge: Attach contrasting color to lower right center front edge and work an additional pattern strip to this edge, joining shell motifs until upper neckline edge is reached. Sew buttons along left button-band edge, to correspond with the first space just below upper shell on right edge, and to correspond with space between every 4th shell down right edge, using these spaces between shell motifs at right edge as buttonholes. See photo.

Band Collar: With right side out, attach dark color between first and 2nd pattern strip at front neckline. Work a row of sc around neckline edge, ending between last pattern strip and button band. Ch 1, turn work, at beginning of each row, and work a total of 7 rows of sc across this portion of neckline, making sure that this sc band measures no more than 15" (15½", 16" across, not counting the button and buttonhole strips, which are not included in the band collar). If sc band measures more than specified above, work decreases by skipping a st at various intervals (across back neckline only, if possible) on 3rd, 4th and 5th rows (or as necessary) until band collar is pulled in to the proper measurement. Complete to 7th row, cut yarn and fasten.

Cuffs: With right side out, attach dark yarn to seam at lower edge of sleeve and work 3 sc through each ch space at base of shell strips, then work 5 more rows sc around to complete cuff. Slip st at seam to join, cut yarn and fasten. Block to desired measurements, taking precautions to prevent dark-colored yarn from running into the light color, or have cardigan blocked to desired measurements by a qualified dry-cleaning establishment.

LACY TRITON SHELL

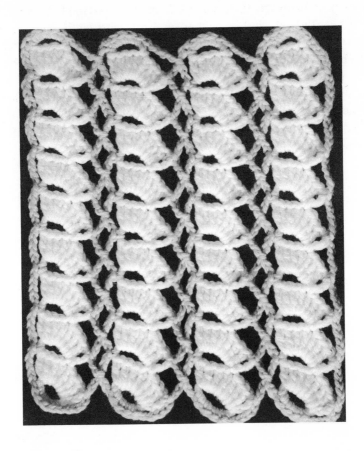

Suggested Uses: Dresses, blouses, bedspreads, afghans, stoles, place setting mats, tablecloths, decorative panels, draperies.

First Strip: Using white (or desired light color) yarn, ch 8, slip st to form ring. Ch 3, 7 dc through ring. *Ch 5, do not turn work, sc in top of 4th dc from left; ch 3, 7 dc through ch 5.* Repeat between *'s until strip is of desired length, and end: Ch 5, sc in top of 4th dc from left. Cut yarn and fasten. Tie colored yarn through last ch 5 made. Sc through chain, *ch 5, sc through space between next 2 shell motifs.* Repeat between *'s along left edge of shell strip to first shell made, ch 5, 5 sc through ch space at base of first shell motif made, *ch 5, sc through ch 3 at edge of next shell motif.*

195

Repeat between *'s along right edge of shell strip to last shell motif, and end: Ch 5, 5 sc through ch 5 at top of strip, slip st into first ch made. Cut yarn and fasten.

Joined Strips: Work as for first strip down left edge and in ch space at base of first shell motif made, then join working strip to completed strip as follows: Ch 5, sc through ch 3 at right edge of first shell motif, ch 2, sc through ch-5 space at left of first shell motif made on completed strip, *ch 2, sc through ch 3 at edge of next shell of working strip, ch 2, sc through ch-5 space at left of next shell on completed strip.* Repeat between *'s until last shell motif of working strip has been joined, and end: Ch 2, sc through ch-5 space on last shell of completed strip, ch 3, 5 sc through ch at top of working strip, slip st into first ch to join. Cut yarn and fasten. Continue joining each strip in this manner until fabric is of desired width.

CANTERBURY COLUMN

Suggested Uses: Afghans, tote bags, ornamental panels, collars, cuffs, edgings.

First Strip: Ch 8, slip st to form ring. Sc through ring. Ch 4, 7 tr through ring; *ch 2, remove hook from loop, insert through top ch of ch 4 (from front to back), insert hook in loop of ch 2 and pull through, sc through ch 2, ch 4, 7 tr through ch-2 space.* Repeat between *'s until first strip is of desired length and end last motif: Pull ch loop through top of ch 4, ch 1, cut yarn and pull through loop on hook.

Joined Strips: Using contrasting color as desired, ch 4, sc through starting ch of previous strip, ch 4, slip st into first ch to form ring. Sc through ring, *ch 4, 7 tr through ch, sc through space above corresponding motif of completed strip (see photo), ch 2, draw ch loop through top of ch 4, as for first strip, sc through ch 2.* Repeat between *'s until strip is the same length as completed strip, ending last motif: Sc through ch 2 of corresponding motif of previous strip, ch 2, pull loop through top of ch 4, ch 1, cut yarn, pull through loop on hook to fasten.

Continue joining strips as above to desired width.

AFGHAN in Canterbury Column Pattern

Size: 40″×60″.

Yarn: 68 oz white (or main color) and 28 oz contrasting color.

Hook: Aluminum size G.

Beginning first strip with contrasting color, work in Canterbury Column pattern, alternating 1 strip of contrasting color and 2 strips of white (or main color), each strip measuring 60″ long. Join strips until afghan measures 40″ wide, ending last 3 strips: 2 white and 1 contrasting color. Add fringe, if desired.

LACY BELL

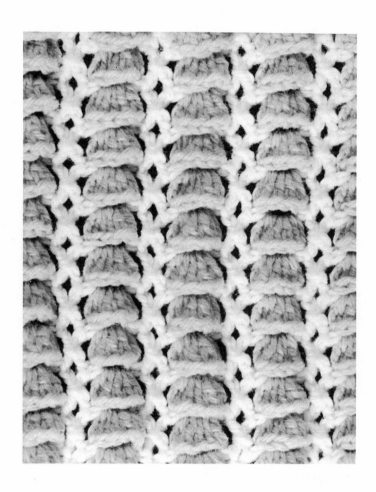

Suggested Uses: Afghans, stoles, lined tote bags, ornamental collars, cuffs, panels.

First Bell Strip: Using color, ch 5, slip st to form ring. Slip st through ch, *ch 3, 6 dc through ch, ch 2, remove hook from loop, insert into top of ch 3 (from front to back), draw loop through, slip st into ch 2.* Repeat between *'s until bell strip is of desired length and end: Draw loop through ch 3, sc through ch-2 space, cut yarn and draw through loop on hook to fasten. Attach white to strand just cut. Sc through ch-2 space, ch 3, sc through space at left hand vertical edge of base of last bell made, *ch 3, sc through space between next 2 bells.* Repeat between *'s along bell strip to first bell made, ch 3, sc through ch-5 space, then repeat between *'s along opposite edge of bell strip, and end: Ch 3, slip st into first white yarn ch made, ch 1, cut yarn and fasten.

Joined Bell Strips: Using color, work second and all succeeding bell strips as for first; attach white and work along 1 edge, as for first strip, ch 3, sc through ch-5 space, then join to completed strip as follows: Ch 1, sc through ch 3 at left edge of first bell made on completed strip, *ch 1, sc through space between next 2 bells of working strip, ch 1, sc through next ch 3 of completed strip.* Repeat between *'s along edge of strip and end: Ch 2, sc into first ch made on working strip, cut yarn and pull through loop on hook to fasten.

Continue to join bell strips to desired width.

AFGHAN in Lacy Bell Pattern
(Not illustrated)

Size: 45"×64".

Yarn: Knitting worsted; 24 oz white and 56 oz color.

Hook: Aluminum size G.

Using color, work first Lacy Bell strip to 64"; change to white yarn and complete strip as directed. Work joined bell strips, each with exactly the same number of bells, until afghan measures 45" wide.

Attach fringe as desired, or work a simple ch st border around all sides.

LACY LEAF STITCH

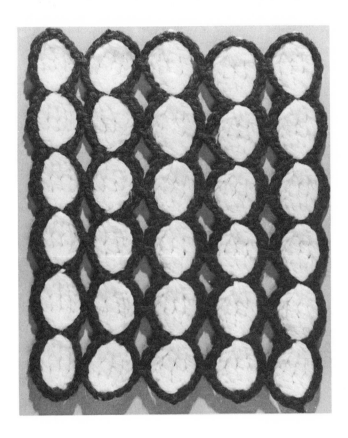

Suggested Uses: Afghans, stoles, place setting mats, bedspreads, tablecloths, ornamental edgings and panels. This pattern makes an attractive stole or coverlet, using 2 or 3 recurring shades of medium to light green for the leaves and a very dark foliage green for the lacy chain portion. For an "Autumn Leaf" afghan, recurring leaf strips can be made with orange, rust brown and light moss green, with a very dark brown or green for the lacy chain portion.

First Leaf Strip: Ch 7; *wrap yarn around hook 3 times, insert through 6th ch from hook and draw yarn through; (yarn over hook, draw through

2 loops on hook) 3 times.* Work between *'s 3 times, then draw yarn through all 4 loops on hook (a leaf made; see photo). Ch 6 and work another leaf in 6th ch from hook. Repeat until leaf strip is of desired length, and end: Ch 1, cut yarn and draw through loop on hook. Tie contrasting color yarn to cut end strand. Sc through tip of leaf; with right side facing, ch 7, sc through strand between first and second leaf, *ch 7, sc through strand between next 2 leaves.* Repeat between *'s down strip to first leaf made, ch 7, sc in tip of leaf and repeat between *'s along opposite side to starting point, ending: Ch 7, slip st into first ch made. Cut yarn and fasten. Mark this last ch edge and join all succeeding strips to opposite side, so that all motifs will run in the same direction.

Joined Leaf Strips: Work another leaf strip and work outline ch down one side, sc in tip of leaf, then attach to completed strip as follows: Ch 3, sc through ch-7 space of completed strip at edge of first leaf made. Ch 3, sc through strand between first and second leaf of working strip, *ch 3, sc through next ch-7 space of completed strip, ch 3, sc through strand between next 2 leaves on working strip.* Repeat between *'s to tip of last leaf and end: Slip st into first ch. Cut yarn and fasten.

Continue joining strips in this manner to desired width.

LACY PUFF STITCH

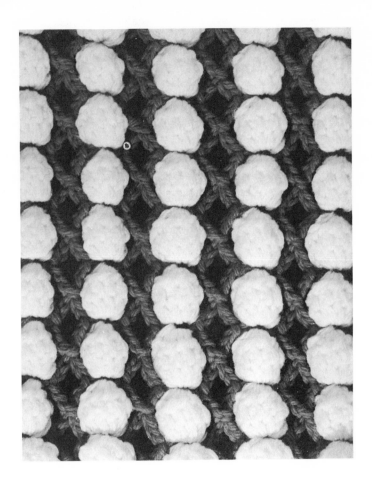

Suggested Uses: Afghans, stoles, lined tote bags, carriage covers, ornamental collars, cuffs, edging, panels. Use leftover yarns with this pattern to make decorative hot mats. Make 2 sides for each mat, working pattern to desired length and width, then place reverse sides together and join with a row of single crochet around outer edges.

First Motif Strip: Using main color, ch 6; holding back last loop of each tr on hook, work 5 tr in 5th ch from hook, then draw yarn through all 6 loops on hook. *Ch 5; holding back last loop of each tr on hook, work 5 tr through strand at tip of motif just completed, then draw yarn through all 6 loops on hook.* Repeat between *'s until strip is of desired length, ending last motif: Ch 1, cut yarn, pull cut end through loop. Turn motif strip to right (puffed) side of fabric. Tie contrasting color yarn to cut end strand; sc in tip of motif. *Ch 5, sc in space between next 2 motifs.* Repeat between *'s down motif strip to first motif made, making sure that puffed side of motif strip is facing; sc in tip of motif, turn strip and repeat between *'s along opposite side to starting point. Ch 5, slip st into first ch made. Cut yarn and fasten. Mark this last ch edge and join all succeeding strips to opposite side, so that all motifs will run in the same direction.

Joined Motif Strips: With main color yarn, work motif strip as before until an equal number of motifs has been completed. Tie contrasting color to cut end strand and work down one side, making sure that puffed side of motif strip is facing, to first motif made (as before); sc in tip of motif and join to completed strip as follows: Ch 2, sc through ch-5 space at edge of first motif of completed strip, *ch 2, sc through space between next 2 motifs of working strip, ch 2, sc through next ch-5 space of completed strip.* Repeat between *'s until last motif has been joined and end: Ch 3, slip st into first ch made. Cut yarn and fasten. Continue joining strips to desired width.

AFGHAN in Lacy Puff Stitch

(Not illustrated)

Yarn: Knitting worsted; 24 oz white and 12 oz each of 4 different colors.

Hook: Aluminum size G (or any size required to obtain the stitch gauge given below).

Stitch Gauge: 3 vertical motifs equal 3"; 4 strips set together equal about 5½" before blocking.

Work first Lacy Puff pattern strip in a color and containing about 65 motifs (or until about 65" long or desired length). Work 2nd, 3rd and 4th joined motif strips each of a different color, and each containing the same number of motifs as first strip, using white to join, until afghan measures 48" across (or desired width). Attach fringe as desired.

STOLE in Lacy Puff Stitch

Yarn: Knitting worsted; 8 oz white and 4 oz each of 4 different colors. The colors used in the photo were pastel turquoise, yellow, pale green and pink.

Hook: Aluminum size G (or any size required to obtain the stitch gauge given below).

Stitch Gauge: 3 vertical motifs equal 3″; 4 strips set together equal about 5½″ wide before blocking.

Work first Lacy Puff pattern strip in a color and containing 62 motifs. Work 2nd, 3rd and 4th joined motif strips each of a different color, with 62 motifs each, and using white to join, until stole measures about 22″ wide. Work a simple ch st border (ch 5, sc in next end ch) across each narrow end and attach fringe of desired length in white, or white with each puff strip containing matching fringe, as shown.

STOLES in Any Suitable Pattern

Stoles are quick and easy to make, forever in style and are exceptionally lovely gifts which the recipient always treasures in a very special way.

Many of the lacy and unusual pattern stitches in Parts III and IV can be used to make stoles in a variety of shapes. The straight one-piece stole can be made in any pattern which has no definite upside-down direction to the casual glance. Patterns with a definite upside-down direction should be made in two pieces and seamed down the center back.

The tapered-back stole and the triangular shawl can be made in any of the joined squares, medallions and motifs, set together as desired. As a general rule, straight stoles should measure about 20 to 22 inches wide and about 64 inches long without fringe, or about 62 inches long when fringe is to be added across the narrow ends. Tapered-back stoles should measure about 32 inches on each side from the angle which forms the neckline portion. Triangular shawls, as a rule, should measure the same length as one's outstretched arms measure from finger tip to finger tip, before fringe is attached; about 61 inches. (See diagrams, pages 210 and 211.)

The amounts of yarn vary, according to whether the pattern used is very lacy or rather closely crocheted. The average amount of knitting worsted or similar needed for most patterns is about 20 to 28 ounces when worked on a size F, G or larger hook. When the pattern is made up of two or more colors, the percentage of a particular color can be estimated. In the lighter weight yarns, such as baby wool and fingering yarn, the amount needed is usually less, varying from about 12 or 14 ounces in the very fine yarns to about 16 or 18 ounces in slightly heavier wools.

Where the pattern is worked with two or more colors, and the amounts needed uncertain, it is a good idea to purchase your materials at a department store yarn counter or needlework shop. Most of these will allow customers to return unbroken skeins of yarn so that one may buy an extra skein or two of each color without fear of having a quantity of unused yarn left over.

Straight stoles can be made without a specific set of directions by working a foundation chain which measures about 21 inches, keeping count of the number of chains worked, then adjusting them to the proper multiple by adding or ripping back to the multiple the pattern requires, or alternatively, making a chain several inches longer than is required, then working the first row of pattern across to the desired width and cutting away the extra length of chain about one-half inch from the end of pattern, and fastening the loose strand. If the pattern is in squares or other joined motifs, simply

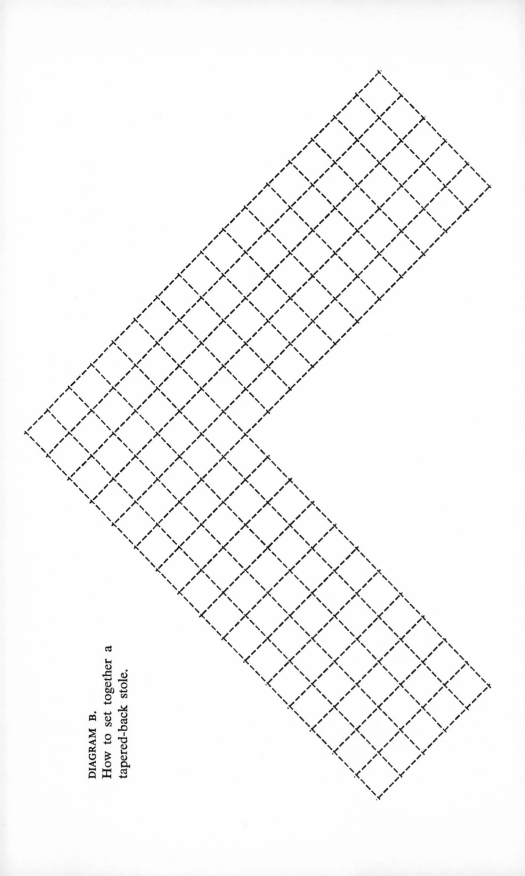

DIAGRAM B.
How to set together a
tapered-back stole.

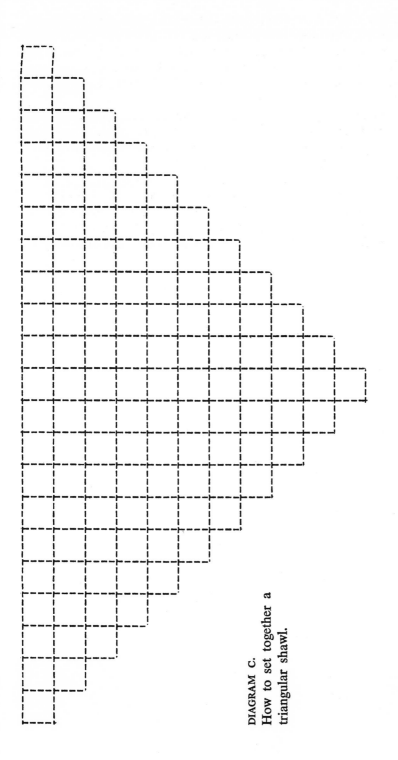

DIAGRAM C.
How to set together a
triangular shawl.

join to the proper width, then proceed with the same number of motifs across each row until the desired length is completed.

Where a pattern has a definite upside-down direction, work two pieces in the same way a one-piece straight stole is made by working in pattern until the piece measures about 32 inches, then make a second piece exactly the same. Sew the pieces together on reverse side with overcast st, making sure that the pattern in both pieces runs the same direction before joining.

These can be finished by working one or two rows of single crochet around entire edge, working 3 stitches in each corner on each row. Add fringe on each narrow edge as follows: For short fringe, cut strands of yarn each 4 inches long. For longer fringe, cut strands 8 inches long. Fold 2 strands in half and pull folded end through first stitch on width edge to form a small loop, using a crochet hook. Pull cut ends through loop, then pull cut ends sharply to tighten. Repeat in each stitch, or at desired intervals, across the 2 width edges. Block or steam press lightly on reverse side.

PETAL STRIPE

Suggested Uses: Stoles, blouses, dresses, afghans, bedspreads, draperies, ornamental panels.

First Strip: Using color A, ch 12. Sc in 8th ch from hook, ch 3, sc in end ch. Ch 5, turn work. Holding back on hook last loop of each tr, skip first ch space and work 3 tr in ch space at left, draw yarn through all 4 loops on hook—a cluster made. (Ch 3, cluster in same space) 2 times, to total 3 clusters in same space, with the 2 ch-3 spaces between. *Ch 4, but do not turn work. Sc in ch 3 at right, ch 3, sc in ch 3 at right, ch 4, sc in ch 5 at right edge, ch 5; in middle ch space work a cluster, ch 3, cluster, ch 3, cluster.* (See photo.) Repeat between *'s for desired length. Cut yarn and fasten.

Second and all succeeding strips: Alternating color B and color A, as shown, ch 7, sc in ch loop at beginning (base) of strip just completed; ch 3 but do not turn work; skip 3 ch, sc in next ch at right, ch 4, sc in end ch at right. Ch 5, skip ch-loop space at right; in ch-loop space at left, work a cluster, ch 3, cluster, ch 3, cluster, *ch 1, sc through ch 5 at edge of completed strip, ch 4 but do not turn work; sc in ch 3 at right, ch 3, sc in ch 3 at right, ch 4, sc in ch 5 at right edge, ch 5; in middle ch space, work a cluster, ch 3, cluster, ch 3, cluster.* Repeat between *'s for same length as first strip, making sure that each strip is counted and contains the same number of cluster motifs as those strips already completed, and end: Ch 1, sc through ch 5 at edge of completed strip. Cut yarn and fasten.

STOLE in Petal Stripe
(Not illustrated)

Yarn: Knitting worsted; 8 oz color A, 8 oz color B.

Hook: Aluminum size G (or any size required to obtain the stitch gauge given below).

Stitch Gauge: Each petal motif should measure approximately 2″ wide and 1½″ long.

Make 2 of the following: Beginning at center back and using color A, work first strip of Petal Stripe pattern until it is about 34″ long. On second strip, use color B and work petal motifs along edge of first strip, as directed, until there are exactly the same number of motifs as in first strip. Continue attaching strips of alternate colors on each succeeding strip until work is about 22″ wide and ending last strip with color A, as for first strip. With right sides together, crochet or sew lower edges together on reverse side to form center back. Block or steam press lightly on reverse side. Attach fringe, if desired. (See flower and fringe card diagrams on last two pages of Part V.)

Part V: CROCHET-HOOK CRAFT:

An Interesting Way to Use

Small Oddments of Leftover Yarns

Flower and Fringe Card Diagrams

Crochet-Hook Craft

Crochet-hook craft is an easy and interesting way for one possessing many crochet hooks of different sizes and various small oddments of leftover yarns to create very pretty decorative flowers. These may be used as applied decoration to a myriad of items, including tote bags, hats, women's wear of all types, pillows, pictures, and perhaps the most interesting creation, very unusual gift package decoration which takes no longer to complete than any other gift-wrapped package one might wish to create.

MATERIALS REQUIRED

Yarns: Most of the items in the following pages are made with very small amounts of various types and thicknesses of yarn, which include acrylic gift-tying yarn, knitting worsted, orlon yarn of knitting worsted weight, bulky and superbulky wool or wool-synthetic blends.

With a little experimenting, almost any leftover yarn may be used for flowers, decorative motifs, etc. In addition to small amounts of the above yarns in various colors, including shades of green and yellow for stems and foliage, a few ordinary household supplies, many of which you may already have on hand, will enable you to make most of the items pictured and perhaps even more from your own imagination.

Assemble the following supplies in a convenient place near a flat working surface:

Metal ruler, 12″ or 18″ length.
Sharp scissors.
White fabric glue which dries clear, with applicator top.
Crochet hooks in the following, or similar, sizes: Steel ⚒0 and ⚒00; aluminum sizes F and G.
Plastic rings in the following sizes: ½″, ¾″, ⅞″, 1″, 1⅛″ outside diameter.
Large plastic comb with both coarse-tooth and fine-tooth sections.
Cotton string of medium weight.
Heavy cardboard.
Hair spray, "hard to hold" or "super hold" type.
Small container of varicolored glitter, with shaker top.

GENERAL DIRECTIONS

Standard methods of making many of the flowers and leaves are given below in lieu of repeating them in each specific set of directions.

Attaching yarn strands to plastic ring: Fold strand in half. Using crochet hook, pull folded end through ring to form a loop about ¾" long, then pull cut ends of the strand through this loop and pull cut ends to tighten.

Combining leaves and flowers to fluff: When using gift-tying yarn, separate the 3 plies in each strand before combing, then proceed as for worsted-weight wool or acrylic, as given below.

When using worsted-weight yarn: Using coarse-tooth section, gently comb strands, beginning at the cut ends, then comb toward base until the plies of yarn are fused into a soft fluff. Run fine-tooth section of comb through fluff 2 or 3 times to smooth and finish, then proceed according to specific directions. NOTE: Save all fluff from combings, separated as to color, in small containers or plastic bags, for use as centers for flowers, which is further explained when fluff is needed in any specific directions making use of it.

Flower center: Using Flower Card ⚹2, cut 4 4" strands of yarn. Place these together and tie tightly in the middle with a 7" piece of string. Separate plies of each strand and trim so that all plies are even, or according to specific directions.

Fluffed yarn center: Proceed as for flower center, then holding string ends firmly, comb all plies into fluff, trimming excess fluff from top, or proceed according to specific directions.

Double-leaf spray: Using acrylic gift-tying yarn and Flower Card ⚹4, cut 2 strands each 6" long. Holding together, tie a firm single knot in the middle of these yarn strands. Separate plies and comb to fluff on each side of knot. Moisten thumb and forefinger and, grasping cut end of fluff, twist into leaf shape, as pictured in photos of finished items. Repeat at other cut end of fluff, completing 2 leaves, one on each side of knot. Trim the tightly twisted strand at end of each leaf to about ⅓", or as directed. Spray lightly with hair spray several times, allowing to dry thoroughly after each application.

Package tie leaf spray: Using separate strands of acrylic gift-tying yarn, tie gift box lengthwise and/or crosswise, according to specific directons, in a firm double knot, leaving 2 5" strands on each side of knot. Separate plies and shape into 2 leaves (as in directions for double-leaf spray, above). Insert a sheet of protective paper underneath leaves and spray lightly 2 or 3 times, allowing to dry thoroughly after each application. Remove protective paper, or proceed according to specific directions.

BASIC TOTE BAGS FOR DECORATING

Cloth tote bag: Size, approximately 13"×14", finished. Materials required: A piece of heavy fabric, suitable for a tote bag, such as monk's cloth, coarse linen or linen type, art burlap, etc., and a piece of iron-on cloth for backing, each cut to 15½"×32". Press iron-on cloth to tote bag fabric, according to manufacturer's directions, making sure that it is firmly bonded over the entire surface of tote bag fabric. Decorate bag as desired, or according to specific directions, allowing 1¼" margin each side for seams and 1¾" margin at each end for hem turn at upper edge of tote bag when finishing. After decoration has been attached, fold bag with decoration side in. Sew 1¼" side seams, and 1¾" hem at upper edge. Attach handle of desired length at upper side seams. Handle may be made of matching fabric, or crochet a chain handle of desired length, using 2 or 3 strands of yarn together.

Crocheted tote bag: Use directions for basic tote bag of double crochet fabric in Part II.

POINSETTIA

Suggested Uses: Decorative motif for holiday floral centerpieces, wreaths, Christmas tree ornaments, gift packages.

Size: 7" diameter.

Yarn: Acrylic gift-tying yarn; 2 yards red and 8" each of lime and yellow.

Flower Card: ✳4 (see page 244).

Hook: Aluminum size G.

All materials and directions not specifically detailed below can be found at beginning of this section ("Materials Required" and "General Directions").

Cut 7 strands of red, each 6" long. Attach each to 1⅛" ring. Comb each double strand into fluff and twist ends of each of these into petals (in the same manner as for leaves), as shown. Spray lightly and allow to dry thoroughly. Using 2 strands of lime and 2 strands of yellow, make a flower center and glue into ring center of lower flower. Spray lightly again and apply glitter to flower center before spray has set.

POINSETTIA Gift Wrap

Materials Required: Gift box of at least 8″ width; dark green acrylic gift-tying yarn, as needed; 1 poinsettia.

All materials and directions not specifically detailed below can be found at beginning of this section ("Materials Required" and "General Directions").

Tie gift box lengthwise and crosswise, as shown, clipping strands 3″ from knot. Comb 2 strands on each side to fluff and twist into 2 leaf shapes. Slip a piece of protective paper under leaves and spray lightly 2 or 3 times, allowing to dry thoroughly each time. Remove protective paper and glue poinsettia to box below leaves, as shown.

STAR FLOWER

Suggested Uses: Decorative motifs for floral centerpieces, holiday wreaths, tote bags, ornaments, gift packages.

Size: 5½" diameter.

Yarn: Acrylic gift-tying yarn; 1¼ yards of desired color.

Flower Card: ⚹3 (see page 243).

Hook: Aluminum size G.

All materials and directions not specifically detailed below can be found at beginning of this section ("Materials Required" and "General Directions").

Cut 7 strands each 5" long. Using a ⅞" ring, proceed exactly as for poinsettia, omitting center, and saving fluff from combing. Spray lightly and allow to dry thoroughly.

Center: Roll a small amount of fluff from combings lightly between palms to form a 1" diameter ball. Flatten ball slightly and spray one side, then apply glitter before spray has set. Allow to dry, then glue back of center in place, as shown. Spray entire flower lightly once more and allow to dry thoroughly.

STAR FLOWER Gift Wrap

Materials Required: Gift box of at least 7″ width; acrylic gift-tying yarn in lime (or desired color) as needed; 1 star flower.

All materials and directions not specifically detailed below can be found at beginning of this section ("Materials Required" and "General Directions").

Using 2 strands together, tie gift box lengthwise, clipping strands 3″ from knot. Comb 2 strands on each side to fluff and twist into 2 leaf shapes. Slip a piece of protective paper under leaves and spray lightly 2 or 3 times, allowing to dry each time. Remove protective paper and glue star flower above leaves, as shown.

STAR FLOWER Tote Bag

Yarn: Acrylic gift-tying yarn; 7½ yards pink (or desired color) for handle; 1⅔ yard lime green (or desired color) for stems and leaves.

Additional Materials: 1 tote bag (see "General Directions"); 3 buttons, about 1½″ diameter; 3 pink star flowers (ring base portion only, with fluff centers omitted).

All materials and directions not specifically detailed below can be found at beginning of this section ("Materials Required" and "General Directions").

Cut 6 strands of pink each 2½ yards long. Place these strands together and tie at one end. Divide into 3 double strands and braid. Tie each end tightly with matching yarn, leaving a 3″ tassel on each end. Cut lime into 3 12″ strands for stems and 4 6″ strands for leaves. Place the 12″ strands together and tie 2 of the 6″ strands about 2″ above one end of the 12″ strands (stems). Tie the remaining 6″ strands around the stems about 2″ above first pair of strands. Comb each single leaf strand on each side of stems into fluff and twist into leaf shape, as shown. Spray flowers and leaves lightly. When dry, glue leaves, stems and flowers to tote bag, as shown, making allowance for seam and upper edge margins of cloth tote bag, if used. If crocheted tote bag is used, slip a piece of foil into bag so that glue will not penetrate to other side of bag. Allow to dry thoroughly. Sew a button to center of each flower with cotton sewing thread, fastening securely on reverse side. Tack stem knots to bag on reverse side. Glue braid to side edges, as shown. When thoroughly dry, tack braid securely in 4 or 5 places along each side to hold.

DAFFODIL

Suggested Uses: Decorative motif for floral centerpieces and arrangements, individual candleholders or taper holders, tote bags, gift wraps, pictures and wall panels.

Size: 4½″ diameter.

Yarn: Acrylic gift-tying yarn; 2 yards for each flower.

Flower Cards: ⚹1 and ⚹3 (see page 243).

Hook: Aluminum size G.

All materials and directions not specifically detailed below can be found at beginning of this section ("Materials Required" and "General Directions").

Base: Cut 10 strands each 5″ long. Attach each to 1″ rings. Comb all strands to fluff, then twist 2 attachments at a time into leaf shape, making 5 petals, as shown. (Daffodils have 6 petals, but for decorative purposes of this item, 5 petals are sufficient.) Flatten slightly and spray. Allow to dry thoroughly.

Trumpet: Cut 4 strands each 3½″ long. Tie together in the middle with an 8″ piece of string. Comb each side to fluff, then grasp string and comb all strands together. Flatten into circle and trim excess fluff from edge. Spray top of this circle heavily, then shape into a daffodil trumpet, as shown, with thumb and forefinger. Spray back of trumpet lightly and flatten outer edge slightly. When dry, trim excess fluff from outer edge of trumpet again, if necessary. Apply glue to inner edge of base at ring. Pull trumpet by ends of string through ring so that base of trumpet is flush with bottom of ring. Reshape trumpet if necessary. Clip twisted ends of petals on base to ¼″. Spray once more, then apply small amount of spray or glue in center of trumpet and apply glitter before glue or spray is set. Allow to dry thoroughly before using.

DAFFODIL Gift Wrap

Materials Required: Small gift box, of about 7″ width; dark green acrylic gift-tying yarn, as needed; 1 daffodil.

All materials and directions not specifically detailed below can be found at beginning of this section ("Materials Required" and "General Directions").

Tie gift box lengthwise on a slant, as shown, clipping cut end strands 3″ from knot. Comb strand on each side of knot to fluff and twist into 2 leaf shapes. Spray entire top of box lightly. Allow to dry, then spray again and apply glitter to leaves and box top before spray has set. Allow to dry, then glue daffodil about 1½″ above leaves, as shown.

JONQUIL

Suggested Uses: Decorative motif for bouquets, corsages, wall panels, pictures, tote bags, gift wraps, individual candleholder or taper holders.

Size: 3½" diameter.

Yarn: See amounts for daffodil, using white or yellow for base, and bright orange for trumpet.

Flower Cards: ⚛1 and ⚛2 (see page 243).

Base: Cut 10 strands each 4" long.

Trumpet: Cut 4 strands each 3½" long.

Proceed exactly as for daffodil, trimming trumpet to 1" length around outer edge.

JONQUIL PICTURE

Materials Required: 1 picture frame, approximately 5½″×7″ inside dimensions; ½ yard dark green (or desired stem and leaf color) gift-tying yarn; small piece of heavy fabric; this may be of single crochet, heavy linen, monk's cloth, etc., to fit inside dimensions of frame; cardboard, 1 jonquil.

All materials and directions not specifically detailed below can be found at beginning of this section ("Materials Required" and "General Directions").

Glue fabric firmly and smoothly to cardboard, which has been cut to fit into frame, and allow to dry. Cut a strand of the green yarn 5″ long, and 2 strands each 3″ long. Tie the 3″ strands across the 5″ strand and comb each side of the 3″ strands to fluff, then twist into 4 leaves, as shown. Glue stem, leaves and jonquil to fabric, as shown. When thoroughly dry, mount in frame.

STRIPED DAISY

Suggested Uses: Decorative motif for floral arrangements, individual candle-holders or taper holders, table centerpieces, gift wraps, holiday ornaments, wall panels, pictures, hats, tote bags.

Size: Small, 2¾" diameter; large, 3½" diameter.

Yarn: Knitting worsted weight; small oddments of yarn in 2 colors.

Flower Cards: ⚞1 for small daisy; ⚞2 for large daisy (see page 243).

Hook: ⚞00 steel.

All materials and directions not specifically detailed below can be found at beginning of this section ("Materials Required" and "General Directions").

Small daisy: Cut 10 strands of color A and 10 strands of Color B, each measuring 3½" long. Attach 2 strands at a time to a ½" ring, alternating colors, as shown. Comb all strands to fluff. Trim excess fluff from around edge. Spray lightly 2 or 3 times, allowing to dry each time.

Large daisy: Cut 19 strands of color A and 18 strands of color B, each measuring 4" long. Attach 3 strands at a time to a ¾" ring, alternating colors and finishing as for small daisy.

STRIPED DAISY Tote Bag

Yarn: Knitting worsted weight; 1 oz blue (or desired color) for handle; 2 yards dark green gift-tying or bulky yarn.

Additional Materials: 1 tote bag (see "General Directions"); striped daisies, 2 large blue and white (or desired color, to match handle), 2 large red and white; 1 small blue and white, 1 small red and white (or desired colors).

All materials and directions not specifically detailed below can be found at beginning of this section ("Materials Required" and "General Directions").

Cut green into 5 strands each 12″ long. Holding all 5 strands together, tie these in a single knot about 3″ from one end. Fold each separate strand in half and tie a single knot about 1½″ from fold, to form a loop (leaf), as shown. Glue these strands to tote bag into position for stems and foliage, as shown. Glue flowers in place. (If a crocheted tote bag is used, slip a piece of foil inside so that glue will not penetrate to back of bag.) When thoroughly dry, tack flowers, stem knots and leaves to bag on reverse side, using cotton sewing thread. If cloth bag is used, finish seams and hem as given in "General Directions."

Handle: Cut blue into 18 strands, each 2½ yards long. Place these together and tie at one end. Divide into 3 hanks of 6 strands each and make a braid about 59″ long. Tie each end tightly with matching yarn, leaving a 2″ tassel on each end. Glue braid to side edges, as shown. When dry, tack braid securely in 4 or 5 places along each side to hold.

PINWHEEL DAISY

Suggested Uses: Decorative motif for pictures, wall panels, floral arrangements, tote bags, gift wraps, individual candleholders or taper holders.

Size: 4″ diameter.

Yarn: Knitting worsted weight; 5 yards main color and 2 yards contrasting color.

Flower Card: ⚹3 (see page 243).

Hook: Aluminum size G.

All materials and directions not specifically detailed below can be found at beginning of this section ("Materials Required" and "General Directions").

Cut 36 strands of main color and 12 strands of contrasting color, each measuring 5″ long. Attach 3 strands at a time to a 1″ ring, alternating 1 contrasting color attachment between every 3 main color attachments. Comb all strands to fluff. Spray lightly, then with finger tips, smooth edge in a counterclockwise direction, creating a pinwheel effect. Spray 2 or 3 times, allowing to dry thoroughly each time. Apply centers as desired.

PINWHEEL DAISY Gift Wrap

Materials Required: Gift box, medium to large; acrylic gift-tying or bulky yarn, 2 yards lime green (or desired color); 2 pinwheel daisies.

All materials and directions not specifically detailed below can be found at beginning of this section ("Materials Required" and "General Directions").

Tie box lengthwise, using 2 strands together. Tie in middle of box with a firm double knot and clip strands 3″ from knot. Comb strands on each side of knot to fluff and twist into 2 leaf shapes. Cut 4 strands each 6½″ long and tie 2 at a time around double strands in a single knot, about 4½″ above and below middle leaves. Comb strands on each side to fluff and twist into leaf shape. Insert a sheet of protective paper under leaves and spray each double leaf spray 2 or 3 times, allowing to dry each time. Remove protective paper and apply glue to each flower at center and press in place, as shown.

LILY

Suggested Uses: Decorative motif for floral centerpieces, holiday ornaments, gift packages; with bulbous center omitted, this flower makes an extremely attractive candleholder or taper holder, as individual holders or in floral arrangements used as table centerpieces.

Size: 4″ diameter.

Yarn: Acrylic gift-tying yarn; 2 yards of desired color for each flower (worsted-weight yarn, used triple strand where 1 strand of gift-tying yarn is called for, may be substituted).

Flower Cards: ✂2 and ✂3 (see page 243).

Hook: Aluminum size G.

All materials and directions not specifically detailed below can be found at beginning of this section ("Materials Required" and "General Directions").

Cut 12 strands each 5″ long and attach 6 of these, one at a time, to a 1″ ring, and the remaining 6 to a ¾″ ring. Comb each attachment on each ring to fluff and twist into leaf shape, as shown. Spray each lightly 2 or 3 times, allowing to dry thoroughly each time.

Center: Cut 3 strands each 4″ long and tie together in the middle with string. Comb each side to fluff, then fold all fibers together and comb again. Twist to bulbous leaf shape, as shown. Spray lightly. Apply glue around 1″ ring and place ¾″ ring on top, so that petals are staggered, as shown. When glue is thoroughly dry, insert string attached to center through both rings and pull so that base of center is flush with lower ring. Spray lightly again and allow to dry thoroughly.

LILY Gift Wrap

Materials Required: Gift box at least 6″ square; dark green bulky or acrylic gift-tying yarn, or knitting worsted used double strand, as needed; 1 lily, white or desired color.

All materials and directions not specifically detailed below can be found at beginning of this section ("Materials Required" and "General Directions").

Using 2 strands of heavier weight yarn or 4 strands of worsted-weight yarn together, tie gift box lengthwise and crosswise, as shown, clipping strands 3″ from knot. Comb strands to fluff on each side and twist into 2 leaf shapes. Make 2 double leaf sprays and glue in place, as shown. Glue lily between leaves, as shown. Spray entire top of box lightly and allow to dry, then spray once more and apply glitter over lily, leaves and top of box, as shown, before spray has set.

CHRYSANTHEMUM

Suggested Uses: Decorative motif for floral centerpieces, tote bags, wall panels, gift wraps.

Size: 5½″ diameter.

Yarn: Acrylic gift-tying yarn; 3 yards main color; 1½ yards contrasting color. (Bulky yarn may be substituted, if desired.)

Flower Cards: ⚡2 and ⚡4 (see pages 243 and 244).

Hook: Aluminum size F or G.

All materials and directions not specifically detailed below can be found at beginning of this section ("Materials Required" and "General Directions").

Cut 12 strands of main color each 6″ long; cut 4 strands of main color each 4″ long. Cut 9 strands of contrasting color each 6″ long. Attach the 6″ strands of main color to 1⅛″ ring. Attach the 6″ strands of contrasting color to ⅞″ ring. Separate plies of all strands on each ring. Apply glue around the 1⅛″ ring and place the ⅞″ ring on top, as shown. With remaining main color strands, make a flower center and pull string through the ring centers so that base of flower center is flush with bottom of lower ring.

CHRYSANTHEMUM Gift Wrap

Materials Required: Gift box of at least 6½″ width; acrylic gift-tying or bulky yarn in 2 shades of green, as needed; 1 chrysanthemum, red and white (or desired colors).

All materials and directions not specifically detailed below can be found at beginning of this section ("Materials Required" and "General Directions").

Using a strand of each color green, tie gift box lengthwise and crosswise, as shown, clipping strands 3″ from knot. Comb 1 strand of each color together to fluff on each side of knot and twist into 2 leaf shapes. Slip a piece of protective paper under leaves and spray lightly 2 or 3 times, allowing to dry thoroughly each time. Remove protective paper and glue chrysanthemum in position below leaves, as shown.

CAMELLIA

Suggested Uses: Decorative motif for floral centerpieces, pictures, wall panels, tote bags, gift wraps, wide-brim hats.

Size: 5½″ diameter.

Yarn: Acrylic gift-tying or bulky yarn; 2 yards color A and 2 yards color B.

Flower Card: ✄4 (see page 244).

Hook: Aluminum F or G.

All materials and directions not specifically detailed below can be found at beginning of this section ("Materials Required" and "General Directions").

Lower part of flower: Cut 5 strands color A and 5 strands color B, each 6″ long. Attach to 1⅛″ ring, alternating colors A and B until all strands have been attached. Comb each double strand into fluff.

Upper part of flower: Make a fluffed yarn center and glue into ring center of lower part of flower.

Trim excess fluff from outer edge of lower part of flower. With finger tips, brush outer edge in a counterclockwise direction, and brush fluffed yarn center in a clockwise direction, as shown. Spray lightly 2 or 3 times, allowing to dry thoroughly each time.

CAMELLIA Gift Wrap

Materials Required: Gift box of at least 6″ width; acrylic bulky or gift-tying yarn, lime green (or desired color) as needed; 1 camellia.

All materials and directions not specifically detailed below can be found at beginning of this section ("Materials Required" and "General Directions").

Tie gift box lengthwise and crosswise, as shown, clipping strands 3″ from knot. Comb 2 strands together to fluff and twist into 2 leaf shapes. Slip a piece of protective paper under leaves and spray lightly 2 or 3 times, allowing to dry each time. Remove paper and glue camellia above leaves, as shown.

FLORAL ARRANGEMENTS

Most of the directions for flowers used as flat decoration may be converted for use in bouquets, corsages, table centerpieces, etc., by using floral wire in desired lengths for stems.

Insert about 1″ of one end of a piece of light floral wire through ring at underside and twist to fasten. Repeat with a second wire on opposite side of ring and twist to fasten, then twist both long ends of wires together to lower ends. Wrap with floral tape from base of flower to end of stem.

Leaves can be attached to flower stems as follows: Cut green gift-tying yarn into 2 strands each measuring 5″. Hold 2 strands together and twist a short section of a 12″ piece of wire around middle of yarn strands to hold firmly. Twist short piece of wire to end. Working 2 strands at a time, comb into fluff and twist ends into leaf shape on each side of wire (see "General Directions" at beginning of this section). Spray lightly and allow to dry. Attach a leaf spray to stems of flowers, as follows: Place leaves 2″ to 4″ below flower (varying length with each flower) and hold both wire stems together. Beginning just under leaves, wrap floral tape around both wire stems to end. Arrange bouquet as desired, folding lower part of stems to shorten each flower to different lengths. Flowers may be sprayed again when arrangement has been completed.

HOW TO MAKE FLOWER AND FRINGE CARDS

Trace flower and fringe card diagrams and transfer tracing to a piece of heavy cardboard. Cut out each card around diagram lines. These cards are then used according to specific directions for flowers (Part V) and fringe.

All of the flowers and leaves herein specifying one or more numbered cards can be made without the aid of the flower cards; however, these are simple to make, and speed up the process of flower making.

With the aid of the flower cards numbered 1 through 4, an enormous amount of time making flowers and fringe can be saved, particularly when directions call for many strands, all cut to a specific length.

Wind yarn around width of card very loosely (to avoid stretching), beginning with cut end of yarn at lower edge. Wind yarn around card once for each strand of yarn required, and end with the second cut yarn end also at lower edge of card. Run scissors blade under all strands of yarn at lower edge of card and cut through these strands.

Flower Card #1 makes strands 3½" long and is used for small striped daisy, daffodil trumpet and jonquil trumpet.

Flower Card #2 makes strands 4" long and is used for flower center, fluffed yarn center, large striped daisy, lily center, jonquil base and 2" fringe.

Flower Card #3 makes strands 5" long and is used for pinwheel daisy, star flower, daffodil base, lily base and 2½" fringe.

Flower Card #4 makes strands 6" long and is used for camellia, poinsettia, chrysanthemum, double-leaf spray and 3" fringe. For 4" fringe, wind yarn around card lengthwise.

DIAGRAM D. Flower Card ⌗1

DIAGRAM E. Flower Card ⌗2

DIAGRAM F. Flower Card ⌗3

DIAGRAM G. Flower Card #4